WISDOM
WITHOUT
ANSWERS
SECOND EDITION

**A GUIDE TO THE EXPERIENCE
OF PHILOSOPHY**

WISDOM
WITHOUT
ANSWERS
SECOND EDITION

A GUIDE TO THE EXPERIENCE
OF PHILOSOPHY

Daniel Kolak

WILLIAM PATERSON COLLEGE

Raymond Martin

UNIVERSITY OF MARYLAND

Wadsworth Publishing Company
Belmont, California
A Division of Wadsworth, Inc.

Philosophy Editor: Kenneth R. King
Editorial Assistant: Karen Jones
Signing Representative: Rochelle Turoff
Production: Ruth Cottrell
Print Buyer: Martha Branch
Designer: Stephen Rapley
Copy Editor: Ruth Cottrell
Compositor: TypeLink, Inc.
Cover Illustration: Barbara Melodia

Excerpt from "Little Gidding" in *Four Quartets*, copyright 1943 by T. S. Eliot and renewed 1971 by Esme Valarie Eliot, reprinted by permission of Harcourt Brace Jovanovich, Inc. Also: Reprinted by permission of Faber and Faber Ltd. from *Four Quartets* by T. S. Eliot.

Printed in the United States of America

1 2 3 4 5 6 7 8 9 10—95 94 93 92 91

Library of Congress Cataloging-in-Publication Data
Kolak, Daniel,
    Wisdom without answers : a guide to the experience of philosophy / Daniel Kolak, Raymond Martin. — 2nd ed.
        p.   cm.
    Includes bibliographical references.
        ISBN 0-534-14598-1
        1. Philosophy—Introductions.   I. Martin, Raymond, 1941– .
II. Title.
BD21.K85   1991
100—dc20   90-41957
                                                                CIP

CONTENTS

PREFACE

We designed this book to be a brief, gripping, and ultimately quite unsettling introduction to philosophy. Our goal is to open questions by moving readers quickly and effortlessly from a position of philosophical naiveté to one of relative philosophical sophistication, so that they are ready and motivated to study philosophy.

Many people come to philosophy with the false impression that it is merely a body of knowledge. They expect to receive information rather than to think for themselves. They often assume they know the answers to many questions that the teacher wants to reopen in a fresh way. Thus philosophers often complain that their students are neither motivated nor ready to grapple with the material used in introductory courses.

This book is designed to solve the problems of motivation and preparation. We show, rather than tell, that philosophy is a questioning and reasoning activity, not a body of information. We engage students in the skills they need to interact critically with the material typically presented in an introductory course. Most importantly, we systematically deconstruct students' attachment to ready-made answers, leaving them ready to make new meaning.

For the second edition we revised the entire book, making many clarifications and additions. We added three new chapters: When, Ethics, and Values, as well as updating and expanding the essay on Further Reading.

We thank all the friends, students, and colleagues who, over the years, have read and commented on earlier drafts

Pojman, Susan Leigh Anderson, Mort Winston, Manuel Velasquez, Marshall Missner, and Wendy Zentz made especially useful comments. We also thank all the people at Wadsworth for doing such a fine job, particularly sales rep Rochelle Turoff; Leland Moss, who served above and beyond the call of duty as production editor for the first edition; Ruth Cottrell, for her skillful advice as production and copy editor for the second edition; and our editor Ken King.

We shall not cease from exploration
And the end of all our exploring
Will be to arrive where we started
And know the place for the first time.

T. S. Eliot, *Four Quartets*

To our students

INTRODUCTION

When we were children we asked questions as children ask them, in complete openness. Where do we come from? What is our purpose in life? What is the nature of the universe in which we live? What happens to us when we die?

We knew we didn't know the answers and we wanted to know them. We didn't assume the questions were unanswerable or beyond our grasp.

As children we were full of wonder. The world amazed us. As adults we have put away our childish curiosity and live within a structure of answers that silences the fundamental questions that have now lost their power to move us. We found answers, but we lost the mystery. How did this happen?

The problem is not with practical answers. We need them to live successfully. The problem is that each of us, as we shall see, has become dependent on a complex interlocking system of metaphysical answers about self, knowledge, reality, values, and meaning. Often these answers are deeply hidden assumptions so basic to our views of ourselves and the world that it is difficult even to realize we are taking anything for granted. Often they are answers to questions we never even asked. Nevertheless, such metaphysical answers, held in place by our desire for security, end up holding us in place. Locked into our answers, we blind ourselves to the fact that the version of reality we experience and believe in is created as much by ourselves, the observers, as by what we observe.

The problem is not just that we interpret our experience. What, after all, is the alternative? The problem is that we interpret our experience in limiting and rigid ways without even realizing it. We thus create a reality more fixed and stable (and inevitable) than any that actually exists. This seeming solidity may make us feel more secure in our beliefs, but such superficial security rests on answers that ultimately hide as much as they reveal. At best, these answers give us knowledge, not wisdom.

Socrates was the quintessential philosopher. He knew just this: that, ultimately, he did not know anything. But he had the skill to show others, no matter how sophisticated or erudite or pretentious, that they too knew nothing.

Socrates used philosophy to call *everything* into question, including even what he took for granted in calling everything into question! He used philosophy—as true philosophers always use it—to show us how to pull the rug out from under ourselves, how to cut through the shield of answers that separates us from the mystery.

The main obstacle to studying philosophy is not that we don't yet know enough. Far from it. It's that we already know too much. This book is designed to remove this obstacle by welcoming you to philosophy in the way that Socrates, if he were here, would welcome you: by pulling you out of your answers long enough to experience the wisdom of unknowing.

We gain little if we merely replace old answers with new ones. The point is to unravel ourselves completely from dependence on answers, to unsettle what has been settled, and to return to an innocent questioning that leaves all security behind and gets its power not from answers but from the unknown.

* * *

An ancient riddle tells of three wise men from three different empires who showed up one day at the gate to a peaceful kingdom. Each had come to seek asylum from the horrible three-way war that, in spite of all their wise advice, had brought their empires to ruin.

The queen of the peaceful kingdom, herself very wise, arrested the three wise men and brought them in chains before an assembly of her people. With all the citizens present, she asked the three wise men why, if they were so wise, they had not been able to prevent their kingdoms from destroying each other.

"The people of each empire, against the advice of their wise men and their emperors, willed that the other empires be destroyed; the emperors had no choice but to comply," said the first wise man.

"The emperor of each empire, against the advice of their wise men and their people, willed that the other empires be destroyed; the people had no choice but to comply," said the second.

"The wise men of each empire convinced the emperors and the people, against their better judgments, that the other empires must be destroyed; the emperors and the people lacked the wisdom not to comply," said the third.

The queen waited for the murmurs that had suddenly arisen throughout the crowd to subside, and then spoke:

"No one shall be a wise man in my kingdom who does not know why kingdoms collapse. So I ask you three wise men, former enemies, to confer among yourselves and decide which answer is correct. If you cannot reach agreement on that, none of you is fit to be wise man in my kingdom, and you will all be beheaded for the crimes you have committed against your own people."

The wise men whispered among themselves for several minutes before coming to a conclusion.

"All three answers are correct, your highness," one of them said.

Again there was a murmur through the crowd.

"You are wise indeed," answered the queen, "but I have no place in my kingdom for three clever enemies who might destroy my people the way you have destroyed your own. So I offer you a choice. Either all three of you leave now, together, free and with my blessing to seek your fortunes and asylum elsewhere. Or you stay. But if you choose to stay, two of you must die.

"The rules are simple. I will ask you to solve a riddle that none of my subjects has been able to solve. The one who solves it first will live as the highest of all the wise men in my empire. The other two will die."

Again, the three wise men, each of whom was convinced that he was wiser than the other two, and each of whom would have liked to see his two enemies dead, quickly agreed. They chose to stay.

The queen blindfolded the three wise men and then painted a dot on each one's forehead. She asked her citizens to take note of the color of each dot and to keep silent about it. The citizens could see that each dot was red. The queen then took the blindfolds off the three wise men and had them face each other.

"I have painted either a red or a green dot on each of your foreheads," she said loudly to the wise men. "Raise your right hand if you see a red dot on at least one of the foreheads facing you."

Because all three wise men had red dots painted on their foreheads, they each saw that the others had red dots painted on their foreheads and so raised their hands.

"Now," ordered the queen, "without talking, and using only the information provided, you must figure out the color of the dot on your own forehead. The first wise man who can do this and then explain how he did it will live."

The first wise man thought: "The other two have raised their hands. Therefore each of them sees a red dot. I can see that they both have red dots on their own foreheads. But they would both raise their hands whether the dot on my forehead was red or green. So there is no way for me to know whether the dot on my forehead is red or green!"

The second wise man thought: "This riddle is unsolvable. If the dot on my forehead is green, I would see what I am now seeing: the other two with their hands raised, and me with my hand raised. If the dot on my forehead is red, I would also see what I am now seeing: the other two with their hands raised, and me with my hand raised. Because the only information I have to go on is the observation that all three hands are raised, and all three hands would be raised whether the dot on my own forehead is red or green, I have no way of determining whether my dot is red or green."

Ten minutes passed. Suddenly the third wise man exclaimed: "The dot on my forehead is red," and then explained to the queen and to the stunned crowd how he knew.

How did he do it?

* * *

Philosophy is not a body of knowledge. It is an activity. Like all activities, it requires skill. What sort of skill? In a nutshell: the ability to see yourself and the world from many different points of view.

What is a "point of view"? Roughly speaking, a point of view is an interpretation that goes beyond the facts and relies on the assumptions, beliefs, or values of the person making the interpretation. For instance, here's a fact: A three-month-old fetus is intentionally aborted. From one point of view, the abortion was murder. From another point of view, it was not murder. The first point of view relies on the following two assumptions: The fetus was an innocent person, and the intentional killing of innocent persons is murder. The second relies on two different assumptions: The fetus was not a person but, at best, a potential person, and the killing of potential persons is not always murder.

In everyday life, we usually get by perfectly well relying only on our own familiar point of view. But even in daily life, especially in times of conflict, the ability to drop our own point of view and see from another point of view can be extremely helpful. In philosophy this skill is more than just helpful, it is essential. Without it we cannot solve problems that are unsolvable within the confines of our own familiar point of view.

* * *

Here's how the third wise man figured out that he, too, had a red dot on his forehead. First, he thought: "There is no way I can figure out the answer by looking merely at what I see from my own point of view. What I see from my point of view would be the same whether my dot was red or green. But the riddle may have an answer. And if it does, and I don't soon discover it, one of the other wise men will, and I shall die. I must, therefore, look for more than what I can now see.

"But what can I look for that I am not now seeing? There are only the three raised hands and the two red dots. If only I could see exactly what Zon and Hsu, the other two wise men, are seeing from their points of view! Perhaps I can. How do things look to Zon and Hsu?

"Zon has a red dot, but he doesn't know it. What he does know is that Hsu has a red dot and that I, Sol, have whatever color dot I have. Suppose, then, that I have a red dot. Then Zon would be in the same predicament I'm now in, namely that of seeing two red dots, and so could not solve the riddle.

"Suppose, then, that I have a green dot. In that case Zon sees that I have a green dot, and that Hsu has a red dot. But if I have a green dot and Hsu has a red dot, Zon would *eventually* be able to figure out that he too has a red dot, for Zon would reason as follows: 'Sol has a green dot, and Hsu has raised his hand, indicating that he sees at least one red dot; because Sol has a green dot, the red dot that Hsu sees must belong to me (Zon). Hence, I (Zon) have a red dot.'

"Hsu also has a red dot, but doesn't know it. What he does know is that Zon has a red dot and that I—Sol—have whatever color dot I have. Hence, Hsu is in exactly the same predicament as Zon. Hence, if I had a green dot, Hsu would *eventually* be able to figure out that he too has a red dot.

"Because ten minutes have elapsed, however, and neither Zon nor Hsu has figured out that he has a red dot, I too must have a red dot!"

At this point Sol informed the queen that he had a red dot, explaining that he came to that conclusion by looking at the situation from the points of view of the others.

The story ends with the beheading of Zon and Hsu and the proclamation by the queen that Sol was now the wisest man in the kingdom. She put special emphasis on the word *man*, and everyone laughed. She then honored Sol by naming the sun after him and offering him any of the royal jewels he most favored.

Sol bowed and thanked her but asked to be given instead the little brush and the can of red paint. He then walked among the crowd and continued on throughout the kingdom, painting red dots on everyone's foreheads as a reminder of what had happened that day.

This all happened a long, long time ago and in a land far, far away and so, of course, most people have forgotten about it. They have also forgotten the lesson that learning to see ourselves and the world from different points of view can sometimes keep us from losing our heads. Perhaps you too will forget. But one day soon you are bound to come across someone with a red dot painted on his or her forehead. And then you will remember.

* * *

Deep inside, we all know that our own points of view are not the only valid ones. But we push this knowledge to the periphery of our consciousness. This leaves us with an uncomfortable, threatened feeling when we are confronted with points of view antithetical to our own. When we admit that our own points of view are based, ultimately, on questionable assumptions, and we thereby lower our shield against alien points of view, we feel insecure. We don't like that. So we allow ourselves to become convinced that our own points of view create the only valid window on the one true reality. Then, when we need to see past the limitations of our own points of view, we get stuck.

The solution, obviously, is to dissolve the glue that binds us to our familiar points of view. Emotional attachment is that glue. And to dissolve it, we must first recognize that all of us rely on questionable assumptions much more than we realize. Second, we must set aside our assumptions and learn to see from other points of view. Finally, we need to integrate the insights we gather from these different, and often conflicting, points of view.

Close one eye, and then the other, several times; you will notice a shift between two conflicting, flat perspectives. Open both eyes and the two perspectives become one unified, three-dimensional vision. Integrating insights from our familiar points of view with insight from even one conflicting point of view gives us binocular vision—a sort of "philosophical depth perception"—that can remove the limitations of living and thinking in flatland.

Having a point of view helps us to see ourselves and the world. But if we become too attached to the answers derived from and sustained by our own point of view, we blind ourselves to other points of view. Thus having a point of view can hide as much as it reveals.

Philosophy shows us how to identify the limitations of our own points of view. But it does more: It teaches us how to get outside ourselves—how to cross the barriers of our familiar framework of answers.

* * *

You're standing at the bank of a river, the deepest and most treacherous river on the planet. Yet you want to get to the other side. How will you do it?

You look for a bridge. There are no bridges.

You try to find a boat. There are no boats.

You want to fly across. There are no airplanes.

In frustration, you search for building materials. There are none.

You consider walking around it, but it flows without interruption all the way from the North Pole to the South Pole.

In desperation, you consider swimming. But the river is too wide and too turbulent. Everyone who has ever entered it has drowned. Yet you want to get to the other side. But how?

When others have tried to tunnel under the river, water swelled up through the earth and drowned them. When they tried draining the river, they discovered that its waters are inexhaustible.

You try everything you can think of. Nothing works. The river is uncrossable. Yet you want to get to the other side. How will you do it?

Don't feel bad if you don't know the answer. The question asks what you should do to get to the other side of a river that's uncrossable. Obviously, you can't cross an uncrossable river.

The answer to the question, "How do you get to the other side of an uncrossable river?" can't possibly have anything to do with crossing the river. The river is uncrossable. Still, you want to get to the other side. How will you do it?

The question appears unanswerable. If the only purpose in asking questions is to answer them, then it is pointless to try to answer an unanswerable question. But is this the only purpose?

Consider an analogy. Could there be any purpose in having weights that you could not lift? It may seem not. Weights tone up your muscles only if you lift them. Isometrics, however, is a system of exercise in which you tone up your muscles not by lifting weights but by exerting your muscles against each other. For example, you clasp the cupped fingers of your two hands together and strain to pull them apart. In isometrics, it is as if you yourself are the weight, and you are trying to lift yourself. You can't do it—but trying to lift yourself can tone your muscles more efficiently than conventional weight lifting.

Isometrics for your body is like trying to lift unliftable weights. Trying to answer unanswerable questions is like isometrics for your mind. Most philosophy is like isometrics for the mind. Throw your hands up in despair before an un-liftable weight and you gain nothing. Throw your hands up in despair before the big, unanswerable questions, and you also gain nothing.

Notice, too, how most of us have been conditioned *not* to ask unanswerable questions. We have been conditioned to assume that there is no point to it. We never consider the possibility that one purpose of asking unanswerable questions might be to tone up your mental muscles. What is more surprising is that there is yet another, even more important, purpose to asking, and to keep on asking, unanswerable questions.

You're standing on the bank of the river. You want to get to the other side. How will you do it? You've exhausted all the traditional answers. What's left? Nontraditional answers. When we are desperate for a solution but the traditional an-swers don't work, we must try nontraditional answers. And to find nontraditional answers to seemingly unanswerable questions, we must drop some of our assumptions about the question and the limits within which it can be answered. Thus trying to answer seemingly unanswerable questions not only strengthens the mind, but also expands it.

Consider the following seemingly unanswerable question: "What is the shortest distance between two points that is even shorter than a straight line?" If you're mathematically sophisticated you know this is unanswerable only within the framework of traditional, Euclidean geometry. If you drop one of the old assumptions about parallel lines—the postulate that two parallel lines can never meet—the question can then be answered within the framework of a non-Euclidean geometry. The answer is: "A curved line."

In other words, questions are neither answerable nor unanswerable *without qualification*. There are no *absolutely* unanswerable questions—absolutely none! There are only *conditionally* unanswerable questions. And there are no *absolutely* answerable questions—absolutely none. There are only *conditionally* answerable questions. Whether a question is answerable or unanswerable depends on the assumptions of the person trying to answer it.

Given the assumptions of Euclidean geometry, the question "What is the shortest distance between two points that is even shorter than a straight line?" is unanswerable. Given the different assumptions of the non-Euclidean geometry of curved spaces, the question *has* an answer.

So how do you get to the other side of an uncrossable river? How do we find answers to questions that, as far as we know, are unanswerable?

We do it by dropping some assumptions. But which? If the river is uncrossable, which assumption could we drop that would get us to the other side? There seems to be just one: the assumption that if you're on one side of a river, you're not already on the other side.

It might seem crazy to drop this assumption, but it's crazy only if we can't imagine how the assumption could be false. We can. Picture the river from space: You see a line extending from the northern tip to the southern tip of a spherical planet. This line is uncrossable. Imagine a point on one side of the line. How could this point get to the other side of the uncrossable line?

It's easy. Imagine that the point faces away from the line and starts walking. Since it never crosses the line and the side of the river it's on extends all the way around the globe, it never leaves its side, yet it gets to the other side. The point doesn't even have to do any walking to get to the other side. Walking didn't get it to the other side. Walking just made it obvious that the point was already on the other side.

The uncrossable line has only one side. The uncrossable river also has only one side. So how do you get to the other side of the uncrossable river?

It's easy. You don't have to do anything. You're already there.

CHAPTER 1

WHERE

Where are you?

Obvious answer: "Here."

Where is "here"?

If you were "here" with us, you would be in Boonsboro. Some of our friends say Boonsboro is nowhere. The map says it's a small town in western Maryland. Maryland is somewhere—on the east coast of the United States. It might be in the northern hemisphere. Or it might be in the western hemisphere. Or perhaps both. We're not sure. It doesn't really matter. What hemisphere we're in depends upon an arbitrary partitioning of the Earth.

Where is Earth? For if we know we're on Earth but we don't know where Earth is, we don't really know where we are. Fortunately, another map tells us Earth is the third planet from the sun in our solar system, our solar system is in an outer arm of the Milky Way galaxy, which is in the Local Cluster of galaxies, which, finally, is in the universe. But where is the universe?

Now there's a question: *Where is the universe?*

Some say the universe is everywhere. But this answer at most locates us *within* the universe. It does not give the universe a location. Suppose you are lost at sea and over the radio a distant voice asks where the sea is. Looking around, you say, "Everywhere." This merely locates you somewhere on the sea. It does not locate the sea. Unless you know what lies beyond the borders of the sea, you are still lost.

So what lies beyond the borders of the universe? Space? No, the universe can't be *in* space, because by *universe* we mean the totality of everything. All space must be in the universe.

Where, then, is the universe? Up to now, we've located each thing by locating it within a containing space. The universe, however, is the ultimate containing space: By definition, the universe contains *everything*. The universe could be somewhere only if there were something the universe did not contain. But there isn't. The universe, therefore, is not anywhere at all; it's nowhere.

If that seems puzzling, consider this. You've probably heard it said that the universe is expanding. What is the universe expanding into, if there is no space beyond it? It seems obvious that if something is expanding, it must be expanding *into* something else. The universe, however, is supposedly expanding without expanding into anything. It's expanding because the distances among the galaxies are increasing over time.

In the distant past, according to many scientists, the entire universe was the size of a pinhead. Where was the space then that is around us now? If the universe was the size of a pinhead, where was the space then that is now Boonsboro, Maryland? Either this space was somewhere in the pinhead universe, or else it was nowhere at all.

So right now we're in a universe that is nowhere! In one sense, of course, we're still somewhere. We're in Boonsboro, Maryland, on the east coast of the United States, in the northern or western hemisphere, on the planet Earth, in our solar system, inside an outer arm of the Milky Way galaxy, in the Local Cluster of galaxies, inside the universe. But, ultimately, *we're nowhere.*

What seems so solidly in place all around us is floating freely in nothing. Ultimately, there is absolutely no support, no foundation, no container, *nothing* to make the whole secure.

Does that make us feel insecure? You bet it does. So we've partitioned the universe not just into galaxies and solar systems and planets and hemispheres and countries and cities, but even down to streets and numbered houses. We can locate each other. We cannot locate the whole. We're still nowhere.

On a huge oceanliner you hear a voice over the intercom: "Folks, this is the captain speaking. I have no idea where we are. We are on a sea that stretches from horizon to horizon,

but I don't know where the sea is. We're completely lost."
Your friend calls you on the phone and says, "Is the captain
crazy? He may be lost. The ship may be lost. But I'm not lost.
I know exactly where I am. I'm on deck 3, cabin 381. I know
where I am."

Your friend's answer might serve some practical purposes.
He might want to have his tuxedo pressed for the evening
ball. But his answer is also a way of shielding himself from
the awesome truth that everyone is lost.

So where are we? Above us there's a sky full of stars.
Below us the Earth. Behind us a mountain. In front, a long
meadow descends into a valley. Woods to the right and left.
We *know* where we are. We're exactly where some of our
friends say we are: nowhere.

Where are you?

CHAPTER 2

WHEN

Here you are, *now*, in the present. When is that? When is the present?

Obvious answer: "Now." The present is "now." But when is "now"?

For us, as we are writing this, it is 9:49 P.M., Eastern Standard Time, Friday, January 5, 1990. We all know when 1990 is: It is the first year in the last decade of the 20th century, at the tail end of a conventionally demarcated one hundred years, twenty-five (or so) centuries after the beginning of Western civilization. When, though, are these centuries?

These twenty-five centuries of history are a small time segment within the approximately fifteen billion year time span that is currently the best estimate of the age of the universe. To comprehend such awesome lengths of time, let us compress the entire fifteen billion years of the universe's existence into one calendar year so that each second corresponds to 475 years, each month represents more than one billion years, and the entire 365 days equals the present age of the universe.

Using this scale, on January 1 the universe "begins." Not until well into the universe's spring, in May, does cosmic debris coalesce, due to gravity, into our local galaxy of stars—the Milky Way. By the end of summer, four months later, our solar system forms out of gaseous remnants while the sun, a seventh-generation star, begins to shine. About one week later, in mid-September, the planetary fireballs cool and become the planets, among them Earth. Another week or so later, in early fall, Earth spawns primitive life in its primordial waters. Not until just before winter, in mid-December, do complex organisms such as fish, land plants, and insects emerge. By the time winter rolls around, in the third week of December, amphibians, reptiles, and trees have appeared, followed, a few days later, by the first dinosaurs. The dinosaurs last three days. As the great reptiles are becoming extinct, the first mammals arrive. On December 30, primates begin to populate the earth.

It is December 31, New Year's Eve, the last day of the cosmic year. Two hours before midnight, at 10:00 P.M., humanoids evolve; at 11:40 P.M., *Homo erectus*, the first primate to walk on two legs; ten minutes later, *Homo sapiens*; at 11:57 P.M., Neanderthals; a minute and a half later, Cro-Magnons. Finally, at 11:58 and 57 seconds, just one minute and three seconds before the present moment, modern humans—*Homo sapiens sapiens*—awaken to find themselves not merely existing but also contemplating their existence.

One minute later, at 11:59 and 55 seconds, philosophy is born. Then, for five fleeting seconds, the entire history of Western civilization, from the ancient Greeks to the present, unfolds.

On the cosmic scale, your entire life—provided you live to a ripe old age—will last almost (but not quite) two-tenths of one second.

So here you are right now, in the present, locating yourself temporally at one end of the fifteen billion years that is the age of the universe. But what about that entire fifteen billion year span, within which all time is located? When is that? In other words, when does the totality of the time that is the duration of the universe occur? *When* does the universe exist?

When *could* it exist? The universe contains not just all of space but, also, all of time. Just as there is no space outside of the universe, so also there is no time. Thus, the universe exists nowhere and never happens.

When does the universe happen? Surprisingly, never. *The universe, which is nowhere, never happens.*

But what about now, what about *right now*? This present moment, when is that? When does it happen? Ultimately, never. Locally, however, we can assign to it a temporal point. For instance, now, as we are writing this, it is 1:11 A.M.,

Saturday, January 6, 1990. When, though, are you reading this? Isn't the present moment in which you are reading this also a now, for you? Isn't it *your* now?

You look at your watch, just as we did. You "see the time." You check the calendar, or your memory, and note the date. You think, "It is no longer 1:11 A.M., January 6, 1990." For you! But for us? Here we are. It is January 6. Our clock says 1:15 already. As we write this, you, the (future) reader (unless you are not yet born) are right now (on January 6, 1990) somewhere probably miles away, perhaps asleep, and you have no idea, at this time (at 1:15 on January 6, 1990), that you will someday (in our future) read this. But you *will* read this. You *are* reading this! Yet, from the perspective of *our* present, the chapter you are now reading is not yet completed. As far as we are concerned, you are not somewhere over there, in the future, reading. You are somewhere over here, in the present, perhaps sleeping.

So where are you? Are you in our future (your present), reading, or in our present (your past), sleeping? And where are we? Are we there, with you, in our future, perhaps teaching, or are we here, as we think we are, in our present, writing? Wherever any of us are, we never find ourselves in the future or in the past but only in the present. For you and for us too the events we experience are going on *now*, in "the present." Yet these different events—your reading and our writing— occur at *different* nows.

We think that our now is really happening and your now has not yet happened. You think that your now is really happening and our now is no longer happening. Who is right? *Which now—yours or ours—is the one actually going on*? Which now is the *real* now?

Ordinary experience suggests a commonsense view about the relation between time and reality: Whatever is going on now is real, and everything real (or fully real) is going on now. You are now having the experience of reading a book. That experience and the book are both real. Even if you were hallucinating, your experience would be real—a real hallucinatory experience. If the book were not really there, your hallucinatory experience of seeming to see the book still would be there. Compare, say, a hallucinatory experience (that someone actually had) of a chair with a merely possible experience (that no one actually had) of a chair. The actual hallucinatory experience, even though hallucinatory, is part of the real world. A merely possible experience (that no one actually had) is not part of the real world (even if it were a possible experience of a real object).

Part of the commonsense view is that anything not in the present is unreal, or at least less real, than whatever exists in the present. The past, we tend to think, is "gone," not merely because past events are not present events, but because past events no longer exist—either at the present moment or at any moment. Past events (such as, from your present point of view, our writing this), although they once existed, do not exist in the present and hence are no longer real.

So, according to the commonsense view of the relation between time and reality, if you remember something you did as a child, the events you remember no longer exist and hence are now unreal (or less real) than your current memory experience of those events. Your current experience, even if a memory experience, exists in the present and hence is real. Similarly with the future. If you know now that tomorrow you will reread this chapter, the event of your rereading it tomorrow is not real until it happens. Until an event happens it is only a mere possibility, not an actuality. And then once the event has happened it vanishes into the past and hence, once again, is not real. In sum, according to common sense, reality resides in the present; past events and future events, since they are not in the present, are not real.

In that case, now, as you are reading these words, our present experience of writing them is no longer real. And, from our present point of view, your experience of reading this is not yet real. Similarly, from the point of view of some future time at which, for instance, you are lying on your deathbed horrified at the thought of your life ending forever, your present experience of reading these words is no longer real. It has been extinguished, with the past, just as you (lying on your deathbed) are about to be extinguished.

Of course, you say to yourself, "But I am not lying on my

deathbed *now*. I am now reading a book." But when you will be lying on your deathbed, you will not say, "There I am now, reading a book." You will say "Here I am now, dying."

When does your death take place? From your present point of view, sometime in the future. From your point of view at the moment of death, your death is happening now. Similarly, from your present point of view, your birth happened in the past. On the other hand, from your mother's point of view at the moment of your birth, your birth is happening now.

But right *now*, as you are reading this, probably you believe that neither the event of your death nor the event of your birth are as real as the present moment. Your birth is over with. Your death has not yet happened. *Now* there is for you only present events, such as your reading this. Since you are reading these words, you are alive. Your life—not your death—is what you think is real. But if the moments in which you were born and in which you will die are just as real—just as real right now (even though those moments are in your past and your future)—then there is a sense (perhaps a profound one) in which even now, as you stare at this page, you are not yet born and you are already dead.

If you are there, in the past, being born, and in the future, dying, then your birth and death and the circumstances surrounding them are somehow fixed. Time, then, would be like a reel of motion picture film, with all moments fully there, all equally real. Each moment, each present, like the individual frames of a movie, is projected so as to give the illusion of a temporal flow. At any one frame (at any one moment) the apparent flow is *from* what you regard as your past *to* what within that same frame (within that same moment) you regard as your future. The reel of film, however, already contains all the frames, all the moments, not just of your life but of all lives, and the apparent flow from past to present to future is but a rapidly flickering illusion.

From within the commonsense view it is difficult to see how all nows might be equally real. Yet, if we pause to think about it, the commonsense view becomes deeply suspect, not because it doesn't seem true but—ironically—because it does seem true! The problem is that the commonsense view seems true at *every* now. But how can every now be the real one when, according to the commonsense view, only the current now (*which* current now?) is the real one?

In other words, at each different moment (at each different now) we feel certain that the now of that moment is the only real one. But this feeling of certainty seems to arise not for any good reason but, rather, merely because we always find ourselves looking outward at all other moments, past and future, from the limited and limiting point of view of a particular now. Viewing ourselves from the perspective of a particular moment blinds us to the genuine possibility that every moment may—at that and every other moment—be equally real.

Suppose we adopt a point of view that abstracts away from our feeling of being located at only one particular moment, at one single now. We might then be able to break the spell of the feeling that binds us to the commonsense view. For instance, suppose you could see the history of the entire universe spread before you, "all at once." What would it look like?

Imagine all the events of the universe spread out like a roll of motion picture film unwound from the reel, left to right, placed flat against a uniform field of light. Gazing down from above along the individual frames you find the event of your birth. Somewhere to the right there is your death, a snapshot moment captured forever in a still frame within the cosmic film. To the left of your birth, dinosaurs graze. To the right of your death, the sun explodes. The sequence of frames (moments) in which we write this (January 5 and 6, 1990) lie to the left of (before) the sequence of frames in which you read this.

What could make it seem from such a bird's-eye-view of the universe that any particular now is any more real than any other? Nothing. Nor would the notions of past, present, and future have the significance common sense accords to them. Ordinarily, by "the past" we mean everything before the present; by "the present," everything "right now"; and by "the future," everything after the present. From the "timeless" perspective, however, there would be no privileged "present" moment relative to which we could demarcate the past from the future. All moments—from the beginning to the end of time—would be there, spread out in eternity, equally present, equally now, equally real.

Which, then, is the real now—ours, as we write this; yours, as you read this; or are all nows equally real (or, perhaps, equally unreal)?

As we write these words it is 5:43 A.M. Eastern Standard Time, Saturday, January 6, 1990. From our point of view, this is now. From your point of view, this (our present now) is then. But from the point of view of the universe as a whole, this now, like your now, like all nows—is nowhere, always and never.

CHAPTER 3

WHO

Who are you?

When someone asks who you are, the obvious answer—your name—pops into your head. You don't have to think about it. But your name is only a name. Your name isn't who you are. The *you* in "Who are you?" doesn't refer to your name. It refers to *you*.

Who, then, are you?

Besides your name, there are your interests, your job, where you live, and so on. But these also are not essential to who you are. You can change your interests or your job or where you live without changing your identity. *You* does not refer to your interests, your job, or where you live. So, again, who are you?

There is your age, who your parents are, all the various things you did from the time you were born until the present moment, what you're like as a person right now, and so on. To which of these, if any, does *you* refer?

What began as a simple request has turned into a complex puzzle. We can't know who you are unless we know to what *you* refers. The obviousness and seeming simplicity of the question "Who are you?" only masks the fact that the reference of *you* is unknown. So let's begin with something about you that *is* known. Let's begin with a question that refers to you and that we can answer. From the answer we may be able to determine the reference of *you*.

One of the most obvious things you know about yourself is your age. So, how old are you?

This time, instead of a name, a number pops into your head almost instantaneously. You don't have to think about it.

The question "How old are you?" is obviously about you.

And you know the answer. So to what does *you* in "How old are you?" refer? The answer that popped into your head was the age of your body. So perhaps *you* refers to your body.

Notice how quickly obviousness flees the moment you confront it! Our ages seem obvious unquestionable facts only because we don't question them.

Your body may be a valid reference of *you*. This conventional reference serves well for many practical purposes. But it is not the only possible reference. For instance, there is the "soul story," according to which *you* refers to an immaterial soul, in which case you could be millions of years old or even infinitely old. And we've all heard the "you're only as old as you feel" story; if *you* refers to how old you feel psychologically or emotionally or intellectually, then you might be either younger or older than your body. Your body may be old, your mind young. Perhaps there's a child in you. Perhaps you're only sixteen. Or ten. Or even younger.

Of course, all of us easily recognize that these alternative numbers rest on stories. Thus when asked our ages, we don't think of any of these alternative numbers. Instead, we automatically give an answer that we assume is a hard fact. We tend to forget that the standard number—the number generated by the hidden assumption that you are the age of your body— also rests on a story because, like every story, the standard way of interpreting our ages includes some make-believe—in this case, that the bodies we have now are the same bodies we were born with.

Look at a picture of yourself as a baby and then look in a mirror. The face in the mirror and the face in the photograph —including the eyes doing the seeing—haven't a single cell in common! The standard way of determining our ages requires us to assume that we are the ages of our bodies and that we have the same bodies throughout our lives. This double-barreled make-believe masks the impermanence of the stuff of which we're made.

By calling assumptions "make-believe" we don't mean they are false (though we allow for that). Rather, we mean, first, that the assumptions are interpretations that go well beyond the data available to experience and, second, that they go beyond the data in such a way that some underlying truth—in this case, the impermanence of the physical constituents of which we are composed—is masked. The masking occurs because these assumption-laden interpretations become so familiar that eventually they generate a feeling of obviousness. This feeling of obviousness then actually alters the way we experience the world. Before we know it, we begin to experience the world—not as the world *is*, independently of our interpretations—but as already colored (sometimes distorted) by our interpretations.

Imagine, for instance, that you're about to go swimming in the Mississippi River. You remember swimming in it as a child. You might assume without question that the river you are about to swim in is the same river you swam in as a child. But the river is made of water, and the water is always changing. Hence the famous aphorism, "You can't step into the same river twice." In one sense the river you swam in as a child no longer exists. All rivers are new. Although we may say that the Mississippi is the same river from day to day, we can all easily recognize that *same* is just a label, *Mississippi* just a name. We know that to get to the truth we have to look beyond labels and names to the actual thing. Naming a river "the Mississippi" and then saying that it is "the same river" from day to day doesn't *make* it the same river, except in a trivial, merely verbal sense. Though we're accustomed to thinking of the Mississippi as the *same* river from day to day, we're really just accepting a convenient story, one which obscures the fact that the reference of the word *Mississippi* is ambiguous. It could refer to the water, the river bank, or possibly something else.

The grammatical structure of the sentence, "Can you step into the same river twice?" is subject–verb–object. The river is the object. We focus on the object and take the subject for granted because we are the subject and we have been conditioned to take our presence in the world for granted. Our own permanence, even more than the permanence of the river, is cloaked in obviousness. So we don't easily see that there are two reasons for thinking that you can't step into the same river twice. The first, obvious one, has to do with the object in question: the river. It leaves *you* completely out of the picture. The second, subtle one, has to do with the subject: you. It puts you into the picture. The first reveals the impermanence of the stuff of which the river is made. The second reveals the impermanence of the stuff of which you are made.

If "same river" refers to the physical parts of which the river is made—the "same water"—the Mississippi of today is not the Mississippi of a few years ago. But to what does the *you* refer when we talk about "the same you"? *If* it refers to the physical parts of which you are made, then, like the river, the *you* of today is not the *you* of a few years ago.

The Mississippi is made mostly of water. It completely renews almost all its water every seven weeks. You are made mostly of cells, each of which is mostly water. You completely renew almost all your cells every seven years. Millions of your cells have been renewed since you began reading this chapter. And as you are reading right now, your atoms are a constant whirlpool of dizzying motion so tumultuous that when you look closely, really closely, at the atoms themselves, the parts of which they are made bubble away from you. You can no more grasp them than you can grasp a handful of water.

Like a river, you too are made mostly of water that is constantly being renewed. But you believe that you, unlike a river, are a continuously existing entity—you are someone. Who?

Again, there is your name. But rivers have names, too. Your name can't be who you are. Your name is only another way of referring to *you*. So who are you, really? We turned to the question of your age to find the reference of *you*. Suppose *you* refers to the actual physical constituents of your present body. The average age of those constituents is no more than seven years. Only your neurons are older. So if you are the age of the constituents of your body, you are no more than seven years old!

Most of your neurons are older than seven years. The constituents out of which your neurons are composed, however— ions, electrons, and so on—are in constant flux. And, in any case, *you* does not refer to your neurons. First, if *you* referred to your *individual* neurons, "How are you today?" would be a question about how your individual neurons are doing. But it isn't. Individual neurons have properties like being long or short, firing or not firing, and so on—not properties like being happy or depressed. The question "How are you today?" is a question about how *you* are doing. The only reason neurons are even worth discussing is that they are a part of your body that has something to do with your mind. If it turned out that your liver retained the same cells over the years, we would not think that *you* refers only to your liver.

Second, if *you* referred to your *collection* of neurons—your brain—then the statement, "You *have* a brain" would imply that your brain has a brain, which is absurd. Furthermore, you could survive (some people actually have survived) the destruction of one entire hemisphere of the brain (provided the remaining hemisphere sustains your full psychology—that is, your memories, personality traits, and so on). If, however, you are your brain, then only about half of you could survive the destruction of one of the hemispheres of your brain—the brain that when complete makes up the totality of you.

In addition, it seems that you could survive the physical replacement of your brain with an exact replica. Consider an analogy. A friend lends you his copy of Beethoven's Fifth Symphony recorded on cassette tape. Using professional recording equipment you make a qualitatively identical copy of that sound structure onto an exactly similar tape. What matters to the preservation of the recorded performance of Beethoven's Fifth Symphony is the music (the sound structure), not the tape on which the music is recorded. Suppose that in the process of transferring the music you accidentally destroy the original tape and so you give your friend the qualitatively identical tape with the newly recorded music on it. If your friend claims that you destroyed the recorded performance of Beethoven's Fifth Symphony which he lent you, clearly he would be mistaken. You merely destroyed the tape on which that performance was recorded. The recorded performance has been perfectly preserved on the new tape.

If the analogy between persons and sound structures is a good one, then what makes you *you* is not neurons—the brain—but, rather, the psychological information encoded on the neurons. Consider, for instance, science fiction dramas in which the entire pattern of someone's brain and body is beamed via teletransporter from a spaceship (where the original atoms are destroyed) to a planet's surface where the exact pattern of the person's entire physical and mental structure is embedded in different, but qualitatively similar, atoms. Nearly everyone regards beaming as a way of traveling from one place to another, not as death with replacement.

Such examples suggest that most people identify not with their atoms (not even with their neurons) but, rather, with the patterns of information encoded on their atoms. It is as if the brain is like a cassette tape on which your personal identity is recorded. Or, perhaps a better analogy (one that includes the active, not just passive, functioning of your mental life) would be to think of your brain as being like the hardware of an extremely powerful and complex computer onto which your personality, thought patterns, memories, and so on—the software —are encoded. Provided the process is accurate, software can travel from one computer to another without loss of identity.

Finally, suppose that tomorrow scientists announce that, contrary to what they previously thought, our neurons are replaced as frequently as the rest of the cells in our bodies— that is, about once every seven years. This would be startling, but no more so than many other discoveries that scientists have already made and the rest of us have readily accepted. Would it shake your confidence in your belief that you survive more than seven years? Probably not. What if scientists discovered that *all* our cells are replaced every seven *months*? Would you then think you live only seven months? Probably not. What if scientists discovered that all our cells are replaced every seven *weeks*? Every seven *days*? Every seven *minutes*? Every seven *seconds*?

As long as such discoveries were about what has always been going on with humans (rather than revealing a way in which human life has suddenly changed), it is doubtful that they would cause us to change our views about how long we survive (or about how we determine our ages). After all, these views originated long ago, when people had no idea that the parts of which they are made are in perpetual flux.

Indeed, individually we each come to view ourselves as being the age of (what we regard as) our bodies before we learn any science. Why, then, when we discover that what we naively thought to be constituted by an underlying permanence (our bodies) is, in reality, constituted by an underlying flux, do we remain attached, without question, to our old (suddenly questionable) view of ourselves as permanent beings? Discovering that what we thought was absolute fact is merely relative to a story, why do we reason (rationalize?) away from the data, rushing toward some new story that preserves our "permanence"? If the method by which we came to believe in our permanence is unreliable, why retain the belief? Why not move to a new view? Is it because our commonsense view of ourselves captures some deeper truth about us (such as that *you* refers, for instance, not to the physical constituents of which you are made but, rather, to your mind), or is it because we (who?) crave permanence more than we crave truth?

Our ages, far from being facts carved in stone, are make-believe stories written on the surface of water. Whoever we are, we are like rivers in that we are composed of impermanent stuff that only appears permanent. We mask this impermanence by attaching ourselves to an interlocking framework of stories—that we are somewhere, that we are someone, that we are the ages of our present bodies, and so on. We *say* our present bodies are older than the physical parts of which they are composed. But isn't this just another one of those underwhelming verbal truths, like the truth that the Mississippi today and the Mississippi one hundred years ago are the same river because we say so?

Perhaps, then, *you* refers to your mind. However, just as your body is not one seamless whole, so your mind is not one seamless whole. Your body is made up of physical parts. Your mind is made up of "mental parts." These "mental parts" are individual mental states: sensations, emotions, and thoughts. If you are the age of your mental states, then how old are you? How old are your sensations, emotions, and thoughts? Perhaps they are the same age as the automatic number you think of when you think of your age. But are they?

Look again at that childhood photograph of yourself. Not

a single atom of a single cell you see in the photograph is still there. The hand holding the photograph and the hand in the photograph haven't a single cell in common. Now ask yourself whether the person in the photograph and the person look- ing at the photograph have a single sensation, emotion, or thought in common.

Do you remember the sensations, emotions, and thoughts going on when the photograph was taken? Do you remember who took the photograph, where you came from to get in front of the camera, where you went after the shutter clicked, and so on? Probably you don't remember many of these things. Just as you once may have believed that your present body and the body in your childhood photograph are the same—in more than a verbal sense—so also you may believe that your present mind and your mind when the photograph was taken are one and the same. But your sensations, emotions, and thoughts have changed even more drastically than did your physical parts. What then makes you believe that you are the same person as the one in the photograph? Isn't that belief based on a story?

Whose story? Isn't it a story made up by the "you-here-and- now" reading these words, the you that, when asked the question "How old are you?", responds automatically with a number—a number that does not really correspond to anything that exists outside of a story? Cloaked in obviousness, our make-believe stories only mask the extent to which our so- called "persistence" is based, ultimately, on impermanence.

For instance, if *you* refers to your mind, how old are you? To answer this, we need to know the age of your mental states—the age of your sensations, emotions, and thoughts. How old are they?

If you're sitting down, focus on the sensation of the pressure of your buttocks against the chair. That sensation is one of your mental states. Here are some others: the sensation of breath passing through your nostrils and into your lungs; the sensation of muscular tension in your fingers and arms as you hold this book; the feeling of anticipation (where is this paragraph leading?) and of yearning (your desire for com- pletion—since thus far we've left you hanging); the changing sensations as you move your body (we are like sharks, constantly in motion); various memories of things you've experienced.

All the sensations, emotions, and thoughts you are now experiencing exist in the present. Even your recalling of a memory, which is *of* the past, isn't itself *in* the past which it recalls. Memories can be experiences only in the present, as sensations, emotions, and thoughts. So, how old are your current sensations, emotions, and thoughts?

To simplify, focus on the sensation of the pressure of your buttocks against the chair. How old is that sensation of pressure? Has it been there as long as you have been physically sitting in your chair? Didn't that sensation of pressure start in the middle of the previous paragraph? Isn't it only (at most) seconds old? Remember that we're not talking about the underlying physical basis for your sensation of pressure. (We have already considered the physical parts of your body.) We're asking about the sensation of pressure itself. It is at most seconds old.

What about your other mental states—how old are they? They too are (at most) seconds old. Just as the face you now see in the mirror and the face in the childhood photograph are composed of qualitatively similar yet different cells, so also the mind looking at the photograph and the mind that was there when the photograph was taken are composed of similar yet different sensations, emotions, and thoughts. You may remember having similar sensations, emotions, and thoughts to those you now have. But those past sensations, emotions, and thoughts are not your present sensations, emotions, and thoughts. For instance, suppose that three years ago you sat on the very same chair sensing the pressure of the seat. You now remember this. That previous sensation of pressure is not the same sensation as your present sensation. The present sensation—the one that now exists—is (at most) seconds old.

What about your memory of that previous sensation? How old is it? The event you remember happened three years ago. That is what people mean when they say a memory is an old one. But, like all your other sensations, emotions, and thoughts, your experience of remembering is (at most) seconds old. Your remembering started as you were reading the second or third sentence of the previous paragraph. It will last (at most) until your attention moves on to something else. Any subsequent remembering of sitting in this chair three years ago will not be *this* remembering. It will be a new remembering. This present remembering—the one going on right now—like all your other sensations, emotions, and thoughts, is itself (at most) seconds old.

So how old are you? If *you* refers to your mind—that is, to your present mental states—the answer is: (at most) a few seconds old.

Remember the famous fountain of youth story? People believed such stories to make themselves feel better about aging. Ironically, what they didn't realize is that there's already a story that goes with the number we think of when we think of our ages. When we drop that story, we find ourselves virtually drowning in the fountain of youth.

Our standard story about our ages may have great practical value. But the standard story misleads us: It makes our permanence and our solidity seem to extend beyond our stories. In doing so, it makes *us* seem to extend beyond our stories. That's why our ages seem like facts carved in stone instead of stories we tell about ourselves. Yet we accept the standard story without question as absolute truth. Why? Isn't it because we crave permanence, solid ground? But who, or what, does the craving? Who are you?

The question is ambiguous. It isn't clear what *you* refers to. *You* might refer to your physical parts or to your mental states. In either case, the foundation for your belief about who you are—that, whoever you are, you are the same person from day to day—is questionable. Just as there is no such thing as a permanent river, except in our stories, so also there is no such thing as a permanent person, except in our stories. Just as all rivers are always brand new, except in our stories, so also all persons are always brand new—except in our stories.

Our stories may or may not be true. But if we don't have good reason for believing them to be true, then (unless we are somehow reliably plugged into the truth) even if we believe our stories and they do turn out to be true, we don't know they are true. And in that case we don't know who we are.

Note that your mental states change much more quickly than does the physical stuff of which you are made. Hence, claiming that *you* refers to physical stuff is analogous to claiming that it's not the water but the riverbanks that make rivers the same from day to day and year to year. The water constantly changes but the riverbanks remain relatively constant.

But even riverbanks flow, just like rivers, only more slowly. You may be more like a riverbank than a river. It depends on whether you anchor yourself to physical stuff—in which case you renew yourself almost completely every seven years—or you anchor yourself to "mental stuff" (sensations, emotions, and thoughts)—in which case you renew yourself almost completely within every seven seconds. Your physical stuff—your cells and atoms—are like riverbanks. Your mental states—your sensations, emotions, and thoughts—are like water.

If it doesn't seem obvious that even the riverbank flows, take a ride on the Mississippi. Don't get off too soon. Go all the way to the end. The waters of the Mississippi empty into the Gulf of Mexico. The banks of the Mississippi empty into the Mississippi Delta. The riverbanks your ancestors may have walked on are now part of the Delta.

When you're visiting the Delta, find a conch shell. Go to a quiet spot and hold the shell to your ear; you will hear what sounds like flowing water. People call it the sound of the ocean, but really it's only the echo of your own blood flowing through your ear canal. It's the sound of you. It's the sound of a river.

CHAPTER 4

KNOWLEDGE

We believe we know a lot. Not just where we are, what time it is, who we are and how old we are, but who our parents are, where and when we were born, how we grew up, where our country is, our planet, our solar system, our galaxy, even where and when the universe is . . . well, at least that the universe is very old and huge and constantly expanding. And of course we certainly know the differences between animals, minerals, and vegetables, what they look like both on the outside and on the inside, what they are made of—for instance, that limestone is made of calcified, marine organisms, that peaches are made of a fibrous, juicy substance, and so on—and we know that ultimately everything is made of atoms. . . .

How do we who ultimately exist nowhere and never and don't even know who we are know so much about everything else?

Most of what we know about ourselves and the world we know only indirectly, on the basis of someone else's say-so. Some of it we know directly, on the basis of our own experience. For instance, you know only indirectly that you have a brain, that the moon has a dark side, that George Washington was the first president of the United States, and so on. You know directly that you are now reading words in a book, that you are breathing, and so on.

Direct knowledge is the ultimate source of all knowledge. Everything that we know indirectly was, at some time, known by someone directly. Otherwise, we couldn't know anything, even indirectly.

For *you* to know something indirectly you have to know it,

ultimately, on the basis of something *you* know directly. For instance, suppose a scientist told you that the east coast of South America and the west coast of Africa used to be connected. You believe her. In doing so, you seem to acquire some indirect knowledge. But how do you know the person who told you is a scientist? How do you know she knows what she's talking about?

Perhaps some university catalog lists her name and characterizes her as a scientific authority on continental drift. But how do you know that the person who told you about the coastlines is the same person named in the catalog? How do you know that what is written in the catalog is true? Even if you did know these things, how do you know that scientific authorities are generally trustworthy? Even if they are, how do you know that *this* scientist, on *this* occasion, is trustworthy?

These questions may seem silly because they raise doubts about whether you know things that obviously you do know. But we're not asking you to deny what you know. We're asking you to explain *how* you know it. In other words, we're not suggesting the scientist doesn't know about continental drift, or that you don't know once she's told you. We're merely asking you to explain to yourself *how* you know. We're trying to get you to see that even if the source of your knowledge is someone else's say-so, and even if that person is an authority, still *you* have to decide whether that person is trustworthy, and ultimately you have to decide this on the basis of things you know directly.

Everything we know indirectly must ultimately be based on things we know directly. So we return to the question: *How* do we know anything directly?

Isn't "experience" the answer? Doesn't all your knowledge—your entire conception of reality, in fact—have to be based on experience? Ultimately—for you—doesn't all your knowledge have to be based on *your present* experience? Everything we know *indirectly* is based on something we know *directly*. And everything we know *directly* is based on our own experience. Everything that anyone ever knows must be based ultimately on the experience of the knower.

You think you know a great deal, not just about yourself,

but also about the whole universe. You think you know what's real, and what's just a fantasy, over an astonishingly large range of topics. Yet everything you know is ultimately based on your experience. Reality seems so solid, permanent, and impersonal, and our experience, when we examine it, is so ephemeral, fleeting, and personal. Yet everything each one of us knows about reality we know on the basis of our own experience.

Consider, for instance, your "knowledge" that the universe is huge, expanding, and billions of years old. Ultimately these "facts" must be known, if they are known, on the basis of experience. If *you* know it, it must be based, ultimately, on *your* experience—even if that experience is only of reading a book.

Suprisingly, it's not just that your knowledge must be based on your experience. Your knowledge must be based on your *present* experience. This means your whole view of reality, including everything you believe you know, must be based, ultimately, on the experiences you are having right now as you read these words!

Suppose, for instance, you think you are eighty years old and have had a lifetime of experiences. You can of course draw upon your past experiences to back up your claims, but first you have to know those experiences really took place. The you-here-and-now reading these words has no *direct* access to any experience that you're not presently having. So how do you know that you've had eighty years' worth of experience? How do you know that the experiences you remember actually took place? Ultimately you have to know all these things on the basis of your *present* experience—in this case, probably your present memories.

You can't know *directly*, on the basis of any *past* experience, that you've had eighty years' worth of experiences. Your past experiences are gone. You may know many things *indirectly* on the basis of your past experiences. To know things *directly* you have to know them on the basis of your *present* experience. How else? Even if you pick up a book of old newspaper clippings, a diary, a photo album, and so on, these things exist in the present. The things you are right now holding in your hands aren't *in* the past. Like your hands, they are in the present. They are here-and-now.

So, there are two kinds of indirect knowledge: knowing something on the basis of *someone else's* say-so rather than on the basis of *your own* experience, and knowing something on the basis of your *past* experience (your present say-so?) rather than on the basis of your *present* experience.

Knowledge about the past must be based on what you know directly in the present. You have no direct access to the past. Whatever you know is based on what you know directly, and whatever you know directly, you must have direct access to. The only thing you have direct access to, however, is *your present experience*. That is why your present experience is the ultimate source of everything you know.

We don't often look carefully at our experience. In this chapter we've begun to do just that. Looking at our experience may seem unusual, but it isn't hard to do. You don't have to know any science or mathematics to do it. You don't have to know anything that you don't already know. It doesn't even take much effort. Looking carefully at your experience is easy.

Once you've looked, it is also easy to see the enormous gulf between your experience and all the things you believe you know about yourself and the world. It's quite astonishing to examine your experience and then compare it even to a radically incomplete list of the things you believe you know. Take a moment to consider your experience right now and compare it to a list of some of the things you believe you know. It's incredible, don't you think, to realize that you know so much on the basis of the experiences you're having right now?

Do you see the incredible gulf between your present experience and what you think you know? If you do, then ask yourself this: If what you're experiencing right now is "here," and all those other things you believe you know are "there," how did you get from here to there? What processes of inference did you employ? What reason do you have for believing those processes of inference are reliable—that they will lead you to the truth, to conclusions that are not just make-believe stories but reality? Do you know the answers to these questions? Does anybody?

One possibility is that science provides the bridge between experience and reality by explaining how experiences are caused. Take, for instance, the experience of watching a sunset. We know directly *that* we have that experience. What we don't know directly is *why* we have that experience rather than some other experience or no experience at all. It is widely believed that the function of scientific theories is to provide explanations of experience. Thus your visual experience of the sunset is explained by the sun's emitting rays of light that travel across space and enter your eyes, sending an electro-chemical impulse along your optic nerve to your brain. If such scientific theories are the best available explanations of experience, then we might be able to legitimately claim that these theories provide the bridge between experience and reality.

There are two problems with this answer. One is with the assumption that scientific theories explain experience. It's not that this assumption is false. The example of the sunset illustrates one of the ways in which scientific theories can at least contribute to an explanation of experience. The problem is that science invariably presupposes the reality of the world "out there" that we were trying to use scientific theories to get to. In other words, science gets us to the reality "out there" by *presupposing* that such a reality exists. That is, science doesn't get us from "here" to "there"; it gets us from "there" to "here."

Furthermore, science doesn't even really get us to "here." Consider again watching a sunset. Nowhere in the scientific explanation of the visual experience of the sunset does science make the link between physical processes and mental experiences. If you look, for instance, in a textbook on the human physiology of our visual system, you will not find any discussion of subjective mental states. What you will find instead are very complicated physicalistic explanations of the way vision works. The closest you'll get to subjective mental states—and usually you don't even get this close—are behavioral reports that people actually make about their visual experiences. But behavioral reports are not themselves subjective mentalistic visual experiences. The gulf is still there. The path from experience to reality remains unknown.

We claimed that all knowledge must be based ultimately on direct knowledge and that all direct knowledge must be based on present experience. If this is true, it seems that it's going to be very hard to explain how we know most of the things we think we know, including most of science. So perhaps one or the other of these claims is false. That could at least save our belief that we have most of the knowledge that we think we have. But at what cost?

If one of our claims about knowledge is false, then either some of our knowledge is *only* indirect or some of what we know directly we know, not on the basis of our present experience, but in some other way. But what could it even mean to have knowledge that is *only* indirect—that isn't based, ultimately, on *any* direct experience? And how could we know something *directly* that we don't know on the basis of our present experience? What, in that case, could be meant by "directly"?

One possibility is that knowledge rests ultimately on assumptions that are not themselves knowledge. In that case, we could know something even though we didn't know it directly. We could know it on the basis of something we merely assumed. For instance, perhaps we could merely assume that memory is generally reliable (even though we don't *know* this) and thereby know all sorts of things on the basis of memory that we couldn't otherwise know. But if we can get knowledge merely by making assumptions, then it would seem that we could know almost anything at all—and effortlessly. This conception of knowledge, it seems, would give us by luck what one should acquire only by honest toil, perhaps cheapening knowledge so much that it would cease being knowledge.

Another possibility is that there is a way of being connected to the truth, and hence of acquiring knowledge, through means other than direct experience. A reliable thermometer, for instance, varies its temperature reading in a way that tracks the correct temperature even though (presumably) it has no direct experience. Perhaps, we too, without knowing it, pulse to the hidden rhythms of reality and thereby acquire knowledge without knowing how or why. We know things not because we know that we know them but because, unbeknownst to us, we are reliably connected to the truth. Although there could perhaps be a kind of knowledge of this sort—knowledge not based on adequate evidence—it would be a sort of "stupid" or, at best, "lucky," knowledge. It would be knowledge without understanding.

Imagine, for instance, that at the end of a semester a new foreign graduate student in mathematics (who as it happens does not yet understand a word of English but has a photographic memory) is registered for an introduction to philosophy course which he has never even attended. His friend, the janitor, who feels sorry for him, steals the professor's exam answers and gives them to him right before the exam, at a time when the janitor knows the math student will surely memorize and use the answers. The math student does not know what the answers mean nor even that they are the answers to his philosophy exam but, just as his friend knew he would, he memorizes them and uses them on the exam anyway.

In giving his answers on the exam, the math student is connected to the true answers as reliably (and as stupidly) as a reliable thermometer. The true/false and multiple choice answers require only the memorization of (what are to him) meaningless letters. The essay questions require the memorization of whole sentences and paragraphs but do not require that the student understands what the sentences and paragraphs mean. In fact, the student has no idea what they mean. Yet all his answers are correct. Thus, when he takes the exam, he gets an "A."

There is a sense in which the student knows all the answers. Indeed, his answers are as correct as the answers that the professor himself would have given! Moreover, if some answers other than the ones the student actually gave had been the correct answers, then the student would have given those (because they would have been the ones written on the copy of the exam answers that his friend, the janitor, would have given him). So, the student is very reliably connected to the true answers and, in that sense, "knows" them. His answers contain no errors, no poor judgments, no infelicities of reason. But his answers are utterly devoid of understanding. If they are knowledge, they are stupid knowledge. They are answers without wisdom.

CHAPTER 5

GOD

A fundamental tenet of many theological systems, both Western and Eastern, is that we can connect directly (and absolutely) to the most real thing: God. According to them, God is the reality underlying the reality of everything, including both experience and the external world. So, if science can't build a bridge from experience to reality, perhaps religion can.

Might the knowledge that God exists provide the necessary bridge between experience and reality—between our subjective mental states and the external world? Perhaps. But only if we know that God exists. Many people believe they know that God exists. But they may be mistaken—even if God does exist. True belief can fail to be knowledge when it fails to be supported by adequate evidence or reasons.

Suppose, for instance, you believe there is life on Mars and your belief turns out to be true. Your true belief might not be knowledge. Your belief might be based not on adequate evidence (such as that a spacecraft brought back samples of life) but on irrelevant considerations (such as that you believe the fourth planet from the sun has life because four is a sacred number). For a belief to be knowledge, the belief must not only be true, it must also satisfy some further condition. The most plausible candidate for such a condition, as we suggested in the last chapter, is that the belief must be based on adequate evidence.

So the question is: Is there *adequate evidence* that God exists? There certainly seems to be: the universe. The mere fact that the universe exists suggests that the universe must have come from somewhere. Everything must come from somewhere.

Tables, chairs, trees, and so on, do not just pop into existence out of nowhere. Tables and chairs are made by people, trees come from seeds, and so on. The universe, too, must have come from somewhere—it must have had an external cause. Everything must have had an external cause. And the only thing that could have caused the universe is God.

But this apparently obvious answer creates an equally obvious problem: If everything must come from somewhere, where does God come from? Perhaps we don't need to explain where God comes from because God, unlike the universe, exists without any external cause. In that case, however, we've blatantly contradicted the very assumption that made us suppose that the universe must have been caused by God— namely, the assumption that everything must come from somewhere. Without that assumption, the existence of the universe is no longer evidence for God.

Perhaps, though, God—unlike everything else, including the universe—does not need an external cause. However, if we're going to assume that God is an exception to this rule, why not just assume the simpler hypothesis that the universe is an exception to this rule? A fundamental tenet of evidence and reasoning is that, all else being equal, the simpler hypothesis should be preferred to the more complex one. The hypothesis that the universe can exist without an external cause requires just one entity—the universe—plus the assumption that the universe is self-caused. The God hypothesis requires *two* entities—the universe and God—plus the assumption that God is self-caused. Thus the hypothesis that the universe can exist without an external cause is simpler than the God hypothesis. Even if it weren't simpler, however, unless we have good reason for adopting one standard for the universe (that is, the universe must have an external cause) and then a different standard for God (that is, God does not have to have an external cause), any conclusion based on such a double standard is not knowledge.

Do we have any reason to adopt one standard for the universe and a different standard for God? Perhaps the universe, because it consists of material objects, requires an external cause. Material objects obviously come into and go out of existence—they are impermanent—and hence are the sorts of things that require an external cause. God, on the other hand, is popularly supposed to be a spiritual being and therefore permanent. So it may seem that God does not require an external cause.

But although it *may* be true that the universe is impermanent, how do we know that it requires an external cause? Indeed, as we shall see in the chapter on nothingness, some scientific evidence indicates that the universe does not require an external cause. So unless someone can establish the limitations of the universe as a whole, it would be simply presumptuous to point to the cosmos and declare it incapable of existing without an external cause.

Furthermore, how do we know that *God*, just by virtue of being a spiritual entity, must be permanent? To know that, we would have to have enough *evidence* about spiritual entities to know their nature. But, as we shall discover (in this chapter as well as the one on death), we don't have such evidence. So if it is presumptuous to claim to know the limitations of the cosmos, it is even more presumptuous to claim to be familiar enough with the nature of spiritual beings to know that God is permanent.

Is there any other possible evidence that God exists? Again, the universe—this time, not the mere fact that it exists, but that it is so well ordered. The precise operation of the solar system, the complex biology of human life, the breathtaking molecular structure of plants—how could all this be the result of mere chance? That it is all mere accident, the result not of design but of the unconscious evolution of matter, would be a fluke too incredible to be believed. We ought, therefore, to believe instead in the existence of an intelligent designer: God.

But if all order, without exception, requires a designer, then God, too, requires a designer. Because if God is supposedly the intelligent designer of the universe, God would have to be even more perfectly ordered than the universe. But if God is even more perfectly ordered than the universe, and God can exist without an external designer, then why not the universe? Claiming that God's order does not require an external designer, whereas the universe's order *does* require it, once more employs an unjustified double standard.

Again, it is tempting to believe that God is special—that God, unlike the universe, does not require an external designer. Maybe God is special in this way. But how can anyone *know* that the universe requires an external designer? And again, as we shall see in the chapter on nothingness, some current theories in physics claim the universe designed itself. What entitles anyone to claim to know *in advance* of examining these theories that they must be wrong? Finally, which is simpler: the idea of a well-ordered universe somehow ordering itself, or the idea of a well-ordered universe plus an even better-ordered (and self-ordered) being who ordered it?

Even if we accept that the universe must be the product of an intelligent designer, what evidence do we have that the designer has the attributes we ordinarily attribute to God? How do we know, for instance, whether the designer is good or bad? We can't usually determine the moral qualities of artists by looking at their paintings. How do we know if the universe had one designer or many? We can't tell by looking at the pyramids how many architects contributed to their design. Indeed, how can we know if the supposed designer or designers of the universe still exist? Watches often outlast their makers.

All the reasons we've considered thus far for the existence of God clearly do not establish that God exists. It is surprising, then, and somewhat disturbing, that these reasons are so often presented *as if* they were good reasons. And there is something even more disturbing about them. The reasons we've considered begin by confronting the mystery in front of our noses—the mystery of the existence and order of the universe around us— and then quickly move in a direction that takes us away both from our experience and from the mystery itself.

The universe is a marvelous and puzzling place that can be observed from your own backyard. The hypotheses we've considered about God do not solve the puzzles but complicate them. Worse, they take you away from the familiar realm of your experience and transport you into the abstract and arcane realm of theological theory. The walls and ceilings of great cathedrals may be beautiful, but you can't see through the windows, and the high vaults obscure the sky. The awesome mystery of the universe cannot be contained in a building—yet any child staring at the open sky can be awestruck.

Is there any other possible evidence that God exists? Numerous holy books not only claim that God exists but also describe God's nature. There are so many holy books, in so many different cultures, separated by great gulfs of time and space; how could there be so many holy books if God did not exist?

If these numerous holy books prove anything about God, however, they prove too much. For not only do they disagree with each other about God's nature, they even disagree about whether God exists. You will find this to be true even if you consider only the holy books associated with the major religions. Theravada Buddhist holy books, for instance, go so far as to claim that God does *not* exist. In any event, even if the holy books agreed with each other, what would that show? By itself, nothing. You can't generate evidence that God exists by taking a vote. At one time almost everybody believed the Earth was flat.

There is, however, one respect in which all the world's holy books are alike: They are all filled with miracle stories that are supposed to provide evidence for the particular religion that the stories help to sustain. However, because the world's religions differ drastically in their beliefs about God, if the miracle stories of one religion count as evidence *for* the claims of that religion, then they also count as evidence *against* the claims of the other religions.

Even if we accept the miracle stories, how do we know to what, or to whom, we should attribute the miracles? If God is responsible, which God? The Hindu God? The Christian God? The Muslim God? For all we know, isn't it possible that the people who supposedly witnessed the miracles caused the miracles themselves through some hidden power unknown even to them? Consider, for instance, so-called miracle cures: Why deny the possibility that we have the power to cure ourselves?

Most people who accept miracle stories in holy books accept only those in *some* holy books. Hindus, for instance, rarely

find the miracle stories in Christian holy books persuasive.
Christians rarely find miracle stories in Hindu holy books
persuasive. Why? Most people who are religious believe in
the religion of their parents. But beliefs that depend on
accidents of birth prove nothing. Just imagine, for instance,
that the Pope's parents had been Hindu rather than Catholic
and that he had been raised in India rather than in the West.
In that case his religious beliefs would probably be different
and he wouldn't have become Pope. He probably would accept
miracle stories he now rejects and reject miracle stories he now
accepts.

For instance, following the long-standing Christian tradition of trying to wean people away from superstitious pagan
beliefs, on a recent visit to Africa the current Pope lectured
Africans on the superstitious character of some of their native
religious practices. He then turned his back to his audience
and celebrated Holy Mass. Suddenly, according to his Catholic
beliefs, the ordinary bread in his hands, through the ritual of
his uttering a few words, literally became the body of Christ,
which he then ate, and the ordinary wine in his chalice literally became the blood of Christ, *which he then drank*! The
Africans were awestruck.

If holy books don't provide adequate evidence that God
exists, what about the personal religious experiences that,
down through the ages and in many diverse cultures, have
been reported by mystics? Many mystics claim to have experienced God. Do their experiences provide adequate evidence
that God exists? It depends on whether the best explanation of
the mystic's experience requires us to suppose that God exists.
If it doesn't, then the mystic's belief that he or she has
experienced God is not knowledge.

Consider an analogy. Many people down through the ages
and in many diverse cultures have had the experience of
apparently communicating with dead relatives. Does the fact
that people have had these experiences prove that ghosts exist? It all depends on whether the best explanation of their
experiences requires us to suppose that ghosts exist. The problem is that there are other ways to explain such experiences:
fraud, hallucination, and so on. For instance, the people might

have hallucinated their communications due to chemical changes in their brains brought on by the shock and grief of losing a loved one. As long as such natural explanations are at least as likely as the ghost explanation, such experiences do not provide adequate evidence that ghosts exist.

So too with the mystic. One way to explain the mystic's apparent experience of God may be to suppose that the mystic actually did experience God. Another way is to suppose that the mystic hallucinated experiencing God only due to chemical changes in the brain brought about by fasting, meditation, or some other unknown but natural cause. So the question is whether we have more reason to believe the mystic's explanation than we have to believe one of these alternative, naturalistic explanations.

We know very little about how the brain works in bringing about our experiences. Dreams, for example, are a form of hallucination. No one knows precisely why dreams occur or why we have exactly the dreams we do. Yet ordinarily we don't suppose that the objects of our dreams are supernatural entities. We suppose that they are merely hallucinations and that somehow or other dreams can be explained naturalistically; we just don't know how yet.

If we don't even know how to explain ordinary dreams, it's not surprising that we don't know how to explain exotic mystical experiences. The fact that we don't know how to explain either sort of experience doesn't mean we won't someday be able to explain such experiences naturalistically. For the mystic's experience to provide adequate evidence for the existence of God, the mystic, or someone, would have to show that the religious explanation of the experience is more likely to be true than that there is some yet unknown naturalistic explanation. No one has ever been able to show this.

Next, we must turn to something we have not yet considered: the possibility of evidence *against* the existence of God. If God exists, why is there so much seemingly unnecessary suffering? God is supposed to be all-knowing, all-powerful, and perfectly good. So either God doesn't know about the suffering (in which case "God" is not all-knowing and therefore not God) or else God knows about the suffering but can't stop it (in which case "God" is not all-powerful and therefore not God). Or perhaps God knows about the suffering and *can* stop it but chooses not to (in which case "God" is not perfectly good and therefore not God).

A possible reply involves an appeal to the concept of free will. God doesn't cause suffering, people do. God chose to create people with free will. What people do with their own free will is their responsibility, not God's. Given a choice between a world in which there is free will and suffering, and a world in which there is no free will and no suffering, the former is the better choice. God made the better choice.

This reply has several problems. First, suffering is often caused not by people but by nature—by so-called Acts of God: floods, earthquakes, tornados, hurricanes, tidal waves, (many) famines, plagues, birth defects, diseases, and so on. Why couldn't we have all the free will we now have without so many natural disasters, and thus without the suffering they cause? It seems strange to suppose that if there were fewer earthquakes, there would *thereby* be less free will.

Second, even with our merely human intelligence, it is easy to imagine how we could have as much free will as we now have without as much suffering as we now endure. For example, God—because God is supposed to be omnipotent— could have created a world in which people are less easily injured. Then, even if people behaved as unwisely as many now do, the consequences would not involve nearly as much suffering. Or God could intervene occasionally to make things go better without interfering with free will. For instance, suppose that God had altered the ocean winds just enough to blow the Conquistadors off course, a small feat in comparison to the creation of the cosmos. What reason is there to think that this Act of God, and the subsequent survival of all those natives of Latin America who were slaughtered mercilessly or died of European diseases, would have resulted in a net loss of free will in the world?

Third, it's not enough to *have* free will. Our free will would have to be of a kind that absolves God of responsibility for our actions. In other words, our free acts would have to be *un*caused by circumstances around us, for instance, by genetic and environmental factors ultimately caused by God. Because if God is behind our actions—if God created a long chain of events that God foresaw would ensure that we do whatever we do—then how could our actions be free in a way that absolves God of responsibility? God at least would have to share responsibility for our actions, because God would have made us perform them.

Furthermore, what evidence do we have that our actions are uncaused? The evidence from psychology and biology suggests that all our actions are caused, ultimately, not by us but by genetic and environmental circumstances. How could anyone claim to know, in light of this evidence, that people have the sort of free will required to absolve God (who, according to religious doctrine, created the genetic and environmental circumstances) of responsibility for our actions?

Finally, an omnipotent God could create a world in which people freely chose to do good rather than evil *as often* as they do in this world. Indeed, God, if God exists, did choose to create such a world: this one. Thus God, it would seem, could also have chosen to create a world in which people freely chose to do good rather than evil *more often* than they do in this world. Such a better world would not be a world without suffering. But it would be a world with *less* suffering. Isn't it possible that it would also be a world with just as much free will as this world? To know that God exists, we would have to have evidence that excludes this possibility. If we can't show that this possibility has been excluded, then God, it seems, is responsible for not having chosen a better world, and hence responsible for the unnecessary suffering in this world. In that case "God" is not God.

We began by asking whether there is adequate evidence that God exists. If there is any such evidence, we haven't yet found it. Perhaps, then, the best response is to appeal to faith. To have faith in God is to believe in God in the absence of adequate evidence. Even many religious experts today concede that there is no adequate evidence for the existence of God and hence that one must believe on faith or not at all. But notice that if the question is whether we can *know* that God exists, anyone who claims that we *must* believe on faith is in effect conceding that the answer is "No." Of course, the Hindu might *claim* to *know* that the Hindu gods exist, just as the Muslim might claim to know that the Muslim God exists, and the Christian might claim to know that the Christian God exists. But on this point—if religious belief is based on faith—the Hindu, the Muslim, and the Christian are all simply mistaken. Faith is not knowledge.

Furthermore, faith cuts both ways. One might just as well believe on faith that God does *not* exist. The believer might appeal to therapeutic considerations, such as that belief in God is psychologically healthier. But many atheists appeal to the same sort of considerations to argue that belief in God is psychologically unhealthy.

Some atheists even claim that belief in God is dangerous, because faith provides no reason for preferring the God of one religion over the God of another. The Hindu, for instance, is just as entitled to believe on faith in Krishna as the Christian is entitled to believe on faith in Jesus, as the Muslim is entitled to believe on faith in Allah, and so on. When people can't settle their fundamental differences rationally, they almost invariably resort to violence. Historically, and even today, religious differences are a potent source of social violence. When people—whether theists *or* atheists—attach themselves more closely to answers than to life, their answers become not solutions but problems.

The believer's response to the mystery of existence is to invoke a mysterious word—*God*. Such a move does little to help us understand ourselves and the universe better. Mysterious words, like mysterious answers, don't solve mysteries. They merely obscure them by putting a verbal barrier between us and the unknown. Such verbal barriers—religious or otherwise—can diminish our feeling of puzzlement at finding ourselves without answers. But there is a big difference between confronting an enigma directly and covering it up. The believer's mystery is a mystery once removed.

CHAPTER 6

REALITY

Theological concepts, like "God," and scientific concepts, like "spacetime continuum," are embedded in elaborate theories developed to explain the reality we experience—the reality we see and feel directly. Reasons for believing in such theories must be based, ultimately, on experience. So rather than using theories as our point of departure (we'll consider them again at the end of the next chapter), let's stick to our experience and see if there is a way of getting from it to an understanding of reality.

Do we directly experience the real world? Most of us believe we do. We may not know who we are or what makes *us* real but we are here, right now, in the universe, experiencing the reality of things like tables and chairs. What makes *them* real?

Take, for instance, an ordinary chair. A chair is one of the most obvious, most concrete, least theoretical, and least controversial examples of a real object. We all know what a chair is. A chair is so familiar to us, so obviously real, that its very obviousness masks the mystery of the chair's reality. If we were talking instead about quarks or black holes, we wouldn't forget the mystery. But because everyone knows what chairs are and that they are real, we assume we all know what it is that *makes* a chair real.

You may be sitting on a chair right now; probably you can see one. Consider the chair. What makes it a real chair? The question isn't what makes it a real *chair*. The question is what makes it a *real* chair—what its *being real* consists of. In other words, the question isn't what makes your chair a real chair as opposed, for instance, to a real table, but, rather, what makes your chair a real chair as opposed to an unreal—a hallucinatory or imagined—chair. If we can understand the reality of a simple object like a chair—what it is that makes it real—then we may be on the way to understanding reality.

This much, at least, seems clear: An unreal chair—a hallucinatory or imagined chair—exists only in our minds. Real chairs exist in the world independently of our minds. So, removing the contribution our minds make to our experience of the chair might help us to understand what makes a chair real. What is that contribution?

To find out, let's look more carefully at our experience. When we experience a chair, we see it, feel it, and think about it. But what is "seeing"? What is "feeling"? What is "thinking"?

The thinking component of your experience is clearly not "out there." Your thoughts may be about something that exists out there independently of your mind, but your thoughts themselves exist only in your mind. Your thought that the chair is comfortable or pretty, for instance, obviously exists only in your mind. Many, perhaps all, of the qualities you attribute to the chair also exist only in your mind. The qualities of comfort and beauty exist only in your mind. Someone else may find the chair uncomfortable and ugly. The chair by itself is neither comfortable nor uncomfortable, neither pretty nor ugly.

Suppose, however, you're thinking that the chair is made of atoms. That thought is obviously in your mind. But the atoms of the chair are not in your mind. Notice, however, that, unless you're looking at the chair through an electron microscope, you don't directly experience the individual atoms of the chair, either. That the chair is made of atoms—even that the dots you see through an electron microscope *are atoms* —is a theory. Ordinarily you don't directly experience the chair as atoms. You directly experience the chair as a chair.

You may be thinking, on the other hand, not that the chair is pretty or that it's made of atoms but, rather, "the chair has the qualities I see and feel directly—the chair is brown, smooth, solid, and so on—and these qualities exist both in my experience *and* in the chair." Is this true?

Before we can find out, we must first clarify what we're

searching for. What might a "mental contribution" to seeing and feeling be like? The idea of such a contribution is unfamiliar. So before we consider qualities such as brownness, smoothness, and solidity, let's first consider a clear, uncontroversial example of how we sometimes, perhaps without realizing it, make a mental contribution to our experience.

As you sit on the chair, you're also seeing and feeling this book. You're looking at this page. Now look at the following word:

Chair

Just look at it. Don't think about it. It may help to look at each letter in the word, left to right and then right to left. Stare at the word for a minute or two without moving your eyes. Blink if your eyes start to water, but otherwise keep your eyes as still as possible and, without thinking, focus right on the word.

What happens? If you look long enough, the word *chair* and its meaning both dissolve into other words and other meanings, like *ha, hair,* and *air,* which then in turn dissolve into the letters *c, h, a, i,* and *r.*

Where then did the word *chair* and its meaning go? Where did the other words and their meanings go? Nowhere. The words and their meanings were never there on the page, existing independently of your mind. You created that illusion by grouping the letters and then assigning a meaning to them. The letters by themselves are not a word. Rather, the word and its meaning are created when you group the letters to create meaning. Meaning is not discovered by you and it does not exist out there on the page independently of your mind. Meaning is made by you and depends for its existence on your mind.

What happens if you keep on looking? First, the letters dissolve into shapes. The *c,* for instance, instead of being a letter, might become a cartoon nose or ear; the *h* might become a chair, and so on. Then, these interpreted shapes further dissolve into uninterpreted shapes—into blots on the page. The letters—which are interpretations of inkblots—were never

"out there" any more than were the "noses" or "ears." The
most that was out there independently of your mind were *uninterpreted* shapes: blots. You're looking at inkblots right now
but seeing letters and words and sentences and thus creating
meaning. But there are only uninterpreted blots on the page.
What binds the blots together and interprets them? You do.

Now consider what happens when you repeat the word
chair silently in your mind. Just say *chair* to yourself over and
over. Don't look at anything—close your eyes. In other words,
do with the sound of the word *chair* in your mind exactly what
you just did with the printed word *chair*. Right now, before you
go on to the next paragraph, spend a minute repeating the
word silently to yourself.

What happens? The longer you listen to yourself repeating
the word *chair*, the more the meaning begins to dissolve. First
the one meaning turns ambiguous—you hear the other words
that compose the word *chair*, like *hair* and *air*. Next, the unity
of that mental sound dissolves as the end of one repetition
slurs into the next. Eventually, all meaning dissolves. You
hear just uninterpreted mental imagery—sounds without
meaning.

The technique of just looking at the written word *chair* and
just listening to the auditory image *chair* separates our
experience of the word *chair* into its components in a way that
reveals the contribution we make to our experience. It makes
clear exactly how our minds can covertly color our experience.

The word *chair*, of course, isn't a real chair. Words are concepts, and concepts depend on our minds for their existence. We
want to know about real chairs—about reality. Is the chair
you actually experience really "out there" or—as seems obviously false—does it, too, depend for its existence on your mind?

Let's examine your experience and find out. Are the
qualities you experience directly properties of your chair?
We've seen that the symbols referring to that chair depend for
their existence *as symbols* on your mind. To what extent, if at
all, do brownness, smoothness, solidity, and so on, depend on
your mind?

Suppose we try to do to your experience of the chair what
we just did to the word *chair* and try to remove whatever

mental contribution you may covertly be making to your experience of the chair. We've already found that just looking at written words dissolves them into uninterpreted inkblots. So let's see what just looking does to your experience of the chair. Just look for several minutes at your chair. What happens?

Your visual experience changes. Just as your visual experience of the written word *chair* dissolved into its component parts, so also your visual experience of the chair dissolves into its component parts. First, your visual experience dissolves into the experience of legs, seat, back, and so on. Then, if you keep looking without thinking and without letting your eyes move, these components of your experience dissolve into further components—ultimately, into colors and shapes. Colors and shapes are all that is left of your visual experience of the chair once your mental contribution has been stripped away. Ironically, it's your eyes and your thoughts *moving* that makes your visual experience of the chair seem so stable.

Ordinarily, when we look at a chair, our experience has a unity and stability. Our experience doesn't dissolve into its uninterpreted components; we don't see just colors and shapes. We see, for instance, a brown leather chair. Why? Because we're not *just* looking. We're looking and thinking. Looking *and* thinking is different from *just* looking.

What we just did to the seeing component of your experience can also be done to the feeling component. First, though, we must separate the seeing and feeling components from each other. Ordinarily, when you look at and feel the corner of your chair, we say you are both looking at and feeling the same thing: the corner of the chair. But this way of speaking obscures the fact that the visual component of your experience—your seeing—is radically different from the tactile component of your experience—your feeling.

What do you *see* directly when you look at the corner of your chair? Ultimately, you see only uninterpreted color patches. What do you *feel* directly when you touch the corner of your chair? Ultimately, only "raw feels"—that is, the uninterpreted experiences of touch, like hot, wet, smooth, soft, and so on. These raw feels are colorless, hence are not color patches. Similarly, color patches are not hot, wet, smooth, soft, and so on, in the way raw feels are. We sometimes use the same language for both visual and tactile experiences. For instance, we say that a color is soft or hot. But the visual experience we call *soft* or *hot* is radically different from the tactile experience we call by the same names.

So color patches are very different from raw feels. And both color patches and raw feels are different from the thing they are experiences of—in this case, the corner of the chair. We obscure these fundamental differences by using the same words to describe all three: color patch, raw feel, and chair. When we are both feeling and seeing the corner of the chair, we say that we are directly experiencing the chair. This is how we forge in our minds the image of reality that we then project onto our experience.

Consider now what happens to your tactile experience of the chair if you *just* feel without thinking—that is, without interpretation. The experience you would ordinarily describe as the experience of feeling your chair, ultimately dissolves into a conglomerate of uninterpreted raw feels.

We rarely *just* look or *just* feel. Ordinarily, thinking—interpreting—is added to the visual and tactile components of experience. What we ordinarily regard as direct experience is thus a mixture, on the one hand, of seeing, feeling, hearing, and so on, and, on the other, of thought. We're so used to both sensing reality and at the same time interpreting it that we don't notice the thinking part—we don't notice the mental contribution we make to our experience.

Experiencing chairs the way we ordinarily experience them, which includes thinking, tends to solidify experience into a concrete image we call "reality." Looking *and* thinking (what we ordinarily call *looking*) or feeling *and* thinking (what we ordinarily call *feeling*) solidify your experience of the chair. Just looking or just feeling dissolves your experience of the chair into its component parts.

What about *just* thinking? Just thinking about our perception of the chair supports the view that most of the qualities we directly experience when we experience the chair are properties not of the chair by itself but depend for their existence on our experience. Think, for instance, about what is going on when you are seeing and feeling the chair. Suppose you see brown and feel solidity. What do you see and what do you feel?

Color is produced by the reflection of light from the surface of the chair. You see "brown," or whatever color your particular chair may be, because the material of the chair absorbs light from some wavelengths and reflects others. The wavelengths that get reflected produce pressure on the back of your retinas. The light stops there. Your eyes are not windows. Your eyes are like radio antennae that pick up wavelengths, convert them into an electrical signal, and then send it along to the receiver. Your brain is the receiver.

The pressure produced by the light on the back of your retina causes electrical impulses to fire along your optic nerve. Your brain receives these impulses and interprets them as brown. The light that produced the pressure is itself uncolored. Light is merely a wave. Just as there are longer and shorter waves on the ocean, so there are longer and shorter wavelengths of light. The difference between "red" light and "blue" light is in the length of the waves. Color is not a property of waves, it depends on the thing interpreting the waves. Your eyes receive the wavelengths, and your optic nerve transmits electrochemical signals to your brain, which then interprets those signals as color.

Thus, on one level, grass can be said to be more "red" than green, because grass absorbs the "red" wavelengths. What you see is what the grass repels: green. On a deeper level, the grass can be said to be colorless. Wavelengths are just that— wavelengths. *We* interpret the lengths of the colorless waves as red, green, yellow, or mauve. Strictly speaking, it's our brains that make such interpretations. Color is not out there— it depends for its existence on us.

What about solidity? You feel the solidity of the chair. But is the chair solid? Perhaps—but consider what the chair's solidity amounts to. The chair is composed of atoms. Between and within atoms there is mostly empty space. If the nucleus of an atom were the size of a marble and placed at the center of the largest football stadium, the electrons would be specks of dust whirling in the uppermost bleachers. Between atoms there is also lots of empty space—even more than between the electrons of an atom and its nucleus. As one famous physicist recently put it during a jam-packed lecture, "The universe is incredibly empty." No one laughed.

We say things like, "You touched a solid chair." But the chair's solidity is questionable, and the closest you get to actually touching the chair is the point at which the force of repulsion between the atoms in your fingers and the atoms of the chair stops your movement. You never directly touch the atoms of the chair. All we ever touch directly is the force of repulsion. Trying to touch, we only repel. We are never in direct contact with each other, or, for that matter, with any object in the universe.

How do the forces you experience when you think you're feeling the chair produce what you call *solid, smooth, warm,* and so on? Just as in the case of color, these forces initiate a complex series of interactions that begin in the tips of your fingers and end in your brain's interpreting those forces to create what we call "experience."

Solidity, color, warmth, smoothness, and so on, are not "out there," independently of your mind. The most that's really "out there" are colorless dots in empty space. Just as you are right now connecting the inkblots on this page, grouping them together to create words and meanings, so you connect the dots you see when you look at the chair, grouping them together in your mind to create colors and solidity. We paint by numbers. But who are we? Are *we* real? What if we, too, are just colorless dots in empty space—space that is itself ultimately nowhere?

What, then, is reality? We began with one of the most uncontroversial examples of a real object—a chair—and tried to understand through examining our experience what it is about the chair that makes it real. On examination, however, we found that none of the components into which our experience of the chair dissolved—seeing, touching, and so on—exist "out there," independently of the mind. Is the answer, then, that the so-called real objects that we directly experience—chairs, tables, and so on—are not "out there" but depend on our minds for their existence?

This may seem too bizarre to be true. Clearly, thought is in the mind. Experience, on the other hand, as we saw, may include a thought component—interpretation—and depend for its existence on our minds. But experience, we ordinarily believe, is caused by something "out there" in the real world that exists independently of our minds and affects our sense organs. Experience, we ordinarily believe, differs from thought in that it provides a kind of bridge between our minds and reality. So perhaps if we understood experience better we might be able to cross that bridge and discover the true nature of reality.

CHAPTER 7

EXPERIENCE

Suppose you burn yourself on the stove. What happens? First there is pain. Then perhaps anger. Then finally the realization that you were careless. The pain is a sensation, the anger is an emotion, and the realization that you were careless is a thought. All three—sensation, emotion, and thought—are components of your experience.

The pain in your finger is clearly a sensation. The thought that you've been careless, on the other hand, seems not to be a sensation. Thinking about burning yourself on the stove, though it might produce discomfort, is different from the actual feeling of burning yourself on a real stove.

What about the emotion of anger? Emotion seems to be a mixture of sensation and thought. Anger at burning yourself is partly a sensation in your body, a feeling of agitation and perhaps of warmth. But it is also partly a thought, in this case (perhaps) the thought that you shouldn't have been so careless.

What, then, is it about experience that makes us think we are in touch with reality? Isn't it the sensation component, which in turn is composed of seeing, hearing, touching, tasting, and smelling? Of the three components of our experience—sensation, emotion, and thought—sensation seems to put us directly in touch with the world "out there," with reality, because, ordinarily, our sensations are directly caused by the actions of real, physical objects on our sense organs.

Sensation may also be colored by our minds—but less, it seems, than either emotion or thought. When you have a sensation, thoughts may be associated with it. But these thoughts are not the sensation itself. You *sense* sensations. You *think* thoughts. You might subsequently think about your pain or your hunger or your pleasure. You're doing that right now— you're thinking about sensations—but you're probably not feeling pain or hunger or pleasure by thinking about these sensations. If you do feel pain, it's because you're actually feeling it, not because you're thinking about it. Pains hurt. Thoughts don't. Or do they?

Can thoughts hurt? Sometimes they can. Suppose you're thinking of the death of a loved one. This thought can cause intense pain. Although a thought isn't itself pain, it can *cause* pain. That's the crucial distinction. Pains are themselves pains. Thoughts aren't themselves pains. If thoughts are painful, it's because they cause pain. But *being* pain and *causing* pain are different.

So does sensation really put us in touch with the world out there—with reality? To see whether it does, we shall have to separate, if we can, those aspects of sensation caused by the outside world from those caused by our own minds. To do that, we must clarify exactly what our sensations consist of. What then does the sensation of pain consist of? This is not a question about what causes pain; nor is it a question about what pain causes. Rather, it is a question about what pain is in and of itself, separate from the things that cause pain and the things pain causes. For example, thought sometimes causes pain, but thought is still distinct from the pain it causes. Similarly, pain sometimes causes thought, but pain is distinct from the thought it causes.

Let's assume, then, that pain is something separate from the things that cause it and the things it causes. What then is pain? We suggested above that pain is one thing and thought another. But is the distinction between pain and thought as neat as that? Perhaps not. Perhaps sensations always include a thought component. And perhaps thoughts always include a sensation component.

It is easy to see that many thoughts have a sensation component. Consider what goes on in your consciousness when you think—for example, when you daydream. Daydreaming is a form of thought. We often think through a problem by daydreaming about it. When we daydream, we make up visual fantasies and watch them unfold. So daydreaming has a sensation component—an internally caused sensation component. But is there anything more to daydreaming than having sensations? It's not clear. But if daydreaming consists just of sensations, then some forms of thinking are just sensations.

Generally, of course, we do not think in visual imagery. Do thoughts devoid of visual imagery also include a sensation component? Often they do. Consider "mental chatter," the kind of thinking you probably do when washing the dishes by hand. When your mind is full of mental chatter, aren't you having a kind of internal conversation with yourself? This doesn't happen just when washing dishes. A great deal of our thinking is internal conversation. Aren't the thoughts that occur during internal conversations usually also imagery—in this case, auditory imagery?

What, though, is an auditory image? Look at the next sentence and then repeat it silently to yourself:

"I am an auditory image."

What you heard in your mind was an auditory image. A great deal of your thinking occurs in the form of auditory images, which obviously include a sensation component—one that is internally, rather than externally, caused. But the experience of auditory imagery is similar to the experience of hearing. The main causal difference is that instead of coming from the outside, auditory images come from the inside. The main experiential difference is that auditory images are usually fainter than external sounds. Mental chatter, then, is also a sensation.

So thought often includes a sensation component. More than that, thought often *is* sensation. Isn't that odd? Thought and sensation seemed distinct enough a few paragraphs ago to make us wonder whether thought *ever* includes a sensation component. But now the relationship between thought and sensation seems so intimate that we may well wonder whether thought is anything *other* than sensation. We'll return to this question shortly.

We have seen that thought is often, perhaps always, just

sensation. Let's see if sensation ever has a thought component. Wouldn't it be interesting to find that sensation often has a thought component? Wouldn't it be strange to discover that sensation just *is* thought? Wouldn't it be bizarre to realize that thought is sensation *and* sensation is thought?

When we considered your experience of the chair, your experience dissolved into two components: sensation and thought. We've now seen that thought often—perhaps always—is sensation. What, then, is sensation?

Consider again the example of pain. You just burned your hand on the stove. You feel a pain in your finger. Pain is among our simplest sensations. Burning your hand on the stove is one of the simplest imaginable examples of pain.

Your finger hurts. This sensation has three distinct conceptual elements: "your," "finger," and "hurt." When your finger hurts, it is *your* finger that hurts, it is your *finger* that hurts, and it is your finger that *hurts*. Aren't "you," "finger," and "hurt" mental concepts rather than sensations? Aren't mental concepts a kind of thought? Let's find out.

Close your eyes and press your right index finger lightly against the cover of this book. What do you feel? Here are some possibilities:

1. You feel your finger press against *Wisdom Without Answers*.
2. You feel your finger press against a book.
3. You feel your finger press against part of the surface of a book.
4. You feel pressure on the tip of your finger.
5. You feel pressure.
6. There is a feeling of pressure.
7. Pressure.
8. . . .

You probably think you feel the first seven items on this list. If you press your finger against the cover of this book, you *should* feel them. But recall that there is a difference between what we actually experience and the interpretation we give to what we actually experience. Assume for the moment that you actually feel pressure on the tip of your finger—the fourth item on the list. Each of the first three descriptions are interpretations over and above the mere fact that you feel pressure on the tip of your finger.

If what you actually feel is pressure on the tip of your finger, then isn't it your mind that interprets that pressure as part of the surface of a book? Then isn't it your mind that interprets that surface as "a book"? And then isn't it your mind that interprets that book as *Wisdom Without Answers?*

Now—was it your finger that experienced the pressure as *Wisdom Without Answers*, or was it your mind? Surely your finger didn't experience the pressure as *Wisdom Without Answers*. Your finger doesn't know how to read! Your mind must have had the experience.

So also with the other information in the first three items on the list. Your finger was affected by pressure, and your mind interpreted the pressure as a book or else as the surface of a book. Aren't books and surfaces of books solid objects? How did your finger know that the pressure was a solid object? Obviously it didn't. Your mind knew the pressure was a solid object.

Therefore, the most you actually experienced independently of your mental contribution was pressure on the tip of your finger. But did you actually experience even that? How could you? How could your finger know that the feeling of pressure was on the tip of your finger? Your finger doesn't have a brain. Your finger can't know anything without your mind's interpreting the pressure as pressure on the tip of your finger.

Once you delete the thought component from your experience, you realize that you did not actually feel the pressure *as pressure on the tip of your finger*. What then? Perhaps you just felt the pressure *as pressure*. Is that what you actually felt? Pressure? Is that what reality is—just pressure?

You did feel a sensation. The only sensation to be felt was pressure. It would seem to follow that you actually felt pressure. Of course you did; but the issue we are discussing is not whether you felt pressure. We are not disputing that you felt it. We are simply trying to separate the sensation component of that experience from the thought component to find out what it is about sensation, if anything, that puts us in touch with reality.

How did your finger know that the sensation was pressure? If your finger couldn't know that the pressure was on the tip of your finger, how could your finger know that the sensation it felt was pressure? Obviously your finger didn't know any such thing. Only minds know. Fingers supply data. Minds interpret data. "Pressure" is part of an interpretation.

What then was the actual, uninterpreted sensation? We have sunk to the bottom of the list, and we still don't know. Perhaps item eight on the list (". . .") is what you actually felt. But what is item eight?

Consider again the example that launched our search: Your finger hurts. Does that sensation have a thought component? Yes. Does your finger know that it is *your* finger? No. Does your finger know that it is your *finger*? No. Does your finger know that the sensation it feels *hurts*? No. How could your finger possibly know any of these things? For that matter, does your finger even feel the sensation of pain?

Notice how closely our experiential account of the thought component of sensation corresponds to the scientific story of what happens when you touch a hot stove. According to the scientific story, the atoms are not white-hot; heat is merely the relative motion of atoms. The energy from this relative motion reaches out beyond the force of repulsion and affects the atoms of your finger. This energy initiates a chain of events that begins at the tip of your finger and ends in your brain. Your nerves send an electrical impulse to your brain. Your brain receives the electrical impulse and *interprets* this impulse as pain.

It may seem, at first glance, that your finger feels the sensation of pain, but—according to the scientific view—it is actually your brain that feels it. Your finger sends an electro-chemical impulse. Your brain interprets this impulse as pain, and this interpretation involves thought.

We have already seen that thought often includes an element of sensation. Perhaps many thoughts are just sensations. Now we see that sensation often includes an element of thought. Perhaps many sensations are just thoughts. What

then is thought? What then is sensation? Could they be one
and the same? The same *what*? Perhaps we have no better
name for it than "experience." But what then *is* experience?

When we looked at the chair, we saw that our experience
dissolved into two fundamental components: sensation and
thought. When we looked at each of these, we saw them re-
unite into one. For lack of a better word, we called this one
thing "experience."

Experience is mind-dependent. But when we think of the
chair that we experience, we think of the chair as something
that exists "out there," independently of our minds. Experience
is ephemeral—it comes and goes from moment to moment. But
when we think of real objects, like chairs, we think of them as
being solid, permanent, and existing wholly independently of
our minds.

We *seem* to experience the chair directly. Yet all we experience directly is our own experience. How, then, does our own
experience, which is impermanent and insubstantial, appear to
be permanent and substantial? In other words, how does the
impermanent become permanent, the insubstantial solid, the
mental concrete?

The two fundamental components of our experience—
sensation and thought—are two different types of the same
impermanent thing. Mixed together they create permanence. In
other words, the relationship between sensing and thinking is
a bit like the relationship between water and cement powder. Water, by itself, flows. Cement powder, by itself, crumbles. Water *and* cement powder, when mixed together, make
concrete.

So it is with sensing and thinking. If you just look, or you
just feel, or you just think, as we did in the case of our experience of the chair, you get something that flows or crumbles.
If you look *and* think, or you feel *and* think, you get the experience of concrete objects—you get chairs.

Now, is the chair you experience—what you see and feel
directly when you look at the chair you are sitting on—a real
chair? We have seen that the chair you directly experience is
a mixture of sensation and thought. Sensation and thought are
both mind-dependent. Reality, we ordinarily believe, is some-

thing that exists independently of our minds. But if sensation—the one component of our experience that contains the least amount of mental contribution from us—can't get us all the way to the reality "out there," what can?

Perhaps thoughts can. After all, it's because we interpret the sensations of things like chairs and books that our experience seems to be of chairs and books rather than simply of pressure. Isn't it our thoughts that, mixed with sensation, lead us to experience reality as stable, permanent, and solid? But where do thoughts come from? Sensations of things like chairs, we think, are caused, ultimately, by the impact of the outside world on our sense organs. That gives sensation some sort of grounding in reality. What claim on reality, if any, do our thoughts have?

If our thoughts are based on nothing—*if* thought is just make-believe—*then* it's hard to see how thought can contribute to experience to get us all the way to reality. We need more than just make-believe stories. If thinking is going to provide the bridge between experience and reality, we need stories that we have some reason to believe are true. We have such stories: scientific theories.

Surely science, if anything, is our bridge from experience to reality. Scientific theories are complex thought structures, but they are not just make-believe. They are thought structures that we have good reason to believe are true. If science is the tree of knowledge, technology is the fruit. Science works. Make-believe doesn't.

Science may provide a bridge from experience to reality but, if it does, it's not to the reality we directly experience. The chair of our direct experience is solid, colored, and stable. Recall, on the other hand, the scientific view of the chair, which we got to just by thinking. That chair is colorless, mostly empty space, and composed entirely of parts that are in constant, violent motion. What happened to the reality we directly experience?

According to science, the reality we directly experience is not reality but make-believe. If science is the bridge from experience to reality, then it's also the bridge from the familiar reality of our direct experience to a reality that is as alien to our ordinary view of ourselves and the world as the most bizarre science-fiction stories. Scientific theories do show us that we can have knowledge that goes way beyond direct experience. But, ironically, one of the things that it seems we then know is that the reality of our direct experience is mostly make-believe. Scientific theories don't pull us out of an abyss in which we are nobody floating freely in nowhere; they push us in.

We've seen that our ordinary view of ourselves and the world is largely a product of thought. This ordinary view has neither the backing of science nor of direct experience. Is our ordinary view of reality, then, merely make-believe? That seems unlikely. After all, we've survived as a species precisely because we've been able to adapt ourselves to the world. If our ordinary view of reality is completely groundless, we wouldn't be here!

But if our being here means we are somehow reliably connected to reality, what is the connection?

We went in search of reality and found several: the subjective reality of our sense experience; the partially subjective, partially objective reality of our ordinary view of the world; and the seemingly objective reality of science. Are these three realities in competition with each other or merely different ways of interpreting the same thing—reality? But what is reality? Because the most obvious examples of real objects are the ones we directly experience—objects like tables and chairs—we turned to experience in the hope of finding out whether it gives us direct access to reality. The answer turned out to be another question: which reality?

Experience, far from giving us direct access to reality, gives us direct access, so far as we know, only to ourselves. It is as if we who are nowhere and know nothing directly except our own experience end up building bridges that lead, ultimately, only back to ourselves.

CHAPTER 8

UNDERSTANDING

We live in a reductionistic age. When we want to understand something scientifically, we explain it in terms of something else that is not that kind of thing. We drop down a level. For instance, we explain minds in terms of living bodies, living bodies in terms of nonliving molecules, and so on.

This reductive strategy has been enormously successful; it has led to unparalleled refinements in our scientific understanding, so much so that our concept of rationality has been molded in its image. The reductive strategy has been so successful that the suggestion that it may have its limitations sounds unscientific and therefore irrational. Yet the very success of this reductive strategy increasingly forces us to face the issue of defining its limits. Two questions, in particular, are unavoidable: "Where, if anywhere, do the reductions end?" and "Have we lost anything along the way?"

The first question asks if the reductive process must somehow eventually bottom out. The second question asks if some things—even if they can be understood reductively—are nevertheless worth understanding on their own terms. The strategy of reductive understanding is a strategy of perpetually changing the topic. So the first question asks if we can continue to change the topic forever. The second asks if—even if we can—we always should.

The first question—Where do the reductions end?—has taken a curious turn in the 20th century. The so-called soft sciences (such as psychology) are in the process of being reduced to the so-called hard sciences (such as chemistry and physics). The extent to which this reduction has been completed is usually considered the measure of scientific progress in the softer sciences. For instance, psychology has been substantially reduced to biology, which has been substantially reduced to chemistry, which has been substantially reduced to physics. Psychology begins by asking "What is mind?" Ultimately, physics answers the question in terms of matter and energy.

But what is physics reduced to? There is no science more basic than physics to which physics can be reduced. So it seems that physics is the end of the line, that physics has the last word, the ultimate answers.

One problem with this reassuring picture is that, during the 20th century, physics hasn't been looking much like the end of the line. A surprising discovery in contemporary quantum mechanics—the most successful scientific theory ever developed—is that at the most fundamental level, mind comes back into the equation. Put in simplest terms:

We ask: What are minds?
We answer: living bodies of a certain kind.

We ask: What is a living body?
We answer: a collection of organic molecules.

We ask: What are organic molecules?
We answer: ultimately, inorganic molecules.

We ask: And what are they?
We answer: collections of atoms.

We ask: What are atoms?
We answer: electrons and neutrons and the like.

We ask: And what are they?
We answer: quarks.

We ask: What are quarks?
We answer: the result of *minds* at work collapsing waves of probability into actuality.

And so once more we ask: What are minds?

In other words, our minds have been reduced to biology, which has been reduced to chemistry, which has been reduced to physics, which has let mind in again through the back door. We began with the question "What are minds?" and we end with the question "What are minds?" We turned away from consciousness in order to follow a reductive strategy that ultimately turned in on itself and led us back again to consciousness. This is Nature's little joke on the 20th century: The reductive process bottoms out by turning back in on itself.

No one knows what this curious situation means for the reductive strategy and for the ideal of rationality that the strategy sustains. The issues here are so technical and the scientific developments so recent that they haven't yet been adequately discussed by philosophers or scientists. So it's too soon to say what this curious knowledge loop means. But it's not too soon to *ask* what it means. It's not too soon to wonder whether it will have profound implications for the future of the reductive strategy and the ideal of rationality that it sustains. It is a real possibility that it will.

Where then does the reductive strategy terminate? We start with mind, and one possibility is that we will end right where we began—with mind. Another is that we will end with some hitherto undiscovered ultimate constituent of everything. Another possibility—and one not to be dismissed, as we shall see in the next chapter—is that we end, literally, with nothing.

What of the second question: Have we lost anything along the way? If there is something that is worth understanding on its own terms and not just reductively, then we *have* lost something. The obvious candidate for what we've lost is the mind in its subjective mode—that is, consciousness or experience. We may be forced ultimately to understand consciousness nonreductively or not at all. But even if we're not forced to understand consciousness nonreductively, that is, experientially, we may derive great benefits from understanding it experientially. When we understand ourselves scientifically, we understand ourselves from the outside, as just another object in nature. When we understand ourselves experientially, we understand ourselves from the inside, as a subject.

What's the difference? The difference is in the *kind* of understanding that results. The difference is between knowing *about* something and simply knowing that thing. When we understand, say, love or anxiety scientifically, we know *about* them. When we understand them experientially we know *them*. We can have the first kind of knowledge even if we've never been in love or experienced anxiety. We can have the second kind of knowledge only if we've had the experience.

A blind person can understand the science of color. Only a person with sight knows what it's like to experience the colors of a sunset. The first kind of knowledge is scientifically rich. The second is experientially rich. They are not in competition with each other. Both sorts of knowledge are essential if we are to understand ourselves and the world fully.

We know that scientific knowledge requires special training. But we tend to assume that experiential knowledge just happens. In a sense it does; in the normal course of living we learn more about life than about physics. But we may not learn much about life. Having an experience and understanding that experience are different things. One does not necessarily lead to the other.

We've already seen where we will end up if we carry the reductive strategy to its limit: either with mind or with some hitherto undiscovered something or with nothing. This last possibility—that ultimately we come face to face with nothing—has already been glimpsed on the horizons of science: Cosmologists trying to understand the origin of the universe have had to face the strange possibility that the universe—which exists nowhere and never happens—came from nothing.

CHAPTER 9

NOTHINGNESS

Imagine nothingness.

No planets or stars. No people. No thoughts or feelings. No matter or energy. No space. No time. Not even emptiness, for emptiness implies a container.

This may be difficult to imagine. So let's start with emptiness. Look around you. You're looking at mostly empty space. All those apparently solid objects are merely configurations of atoms, which are themselves mostly empty space. Furthermore, "solid" objects are a scarcity. The universe contains much more empty space than matter. In the vast distances between stars there is on the average only one subatomic particle per square kilometer of space.

So the universe has very little matter; in fact, the ratio of matter to empty space is about one part to a billion. If we applied U.S. government standards for determining the amount of salt in food to the question of how much matter there is in the universe, we would conclude that the universe is matter-free.

Thus you don't have to do much to imagine emptiness. Emptiness surrounded by emptiness is what we are. Emptiness is close to nothing. So if you want to get an approximate idea of what nothing looks like, just look around! Look toward the heavens. Look around your living room. Look in a mirror. *Everything you see is almost nothing.*

Thus the universe, which is nowhere and never, is mostly empty space, and empty space is close to nothing. Yet *something* exists. We might not be sure what it is, but it's not just nothing.

Why isn't there *just* nothing? Why does anything at all exist rather than nothing?

One old answer is that God created the universe. That might take care of the universe. But what about God? God, we are told, has always existed without beginning or end. God is responsible for the existence of both space and time but is not anywhere *in* space and time.

If God created the universe, then the universe exists because God created it. That doesn't explain why God exists. God is not nothing; God, too—whether God is a thing or not—is something. So the old religious answer merely pushes the question of why there is something rather than nothing one step further back. It does not answer the question. For now we must ask: Why God rather than nothing?

To answer the question of why anything at all exists rather than nothing, religion would also have to explain why God exists. If there is no reason why God exists, then ultimately religion can't explain why something exists rather than nothing.

Can religion explain why God exists? One possibility is that God has always existed. Suppose that's true. Would that explain why something—in this case God—exists rather than nothing?

No. The claim that God has always existed tells us *that* God has always existed, but not *why* God has always existed. To answer the question of why something exists rather than nothing, religion would have to explain why God exists.

Some theologians believe this question doesn't have an answer, or that, if it does have an answer, we can't know what it is. They believe God is beyond reason. These theologians, therefore, would have to concede that ultimately there is no knowable answer to the question of why something exists rather than nothing. Other theologians believe that there is a reason why God exists: It is not possible for God *not* to exist, because the very nature of God ensures that God exists. God exists because God has to exist. God exists necessarily.

These latter theologians claim that the universe—unlike God—does not exist necessarily. They claim that if it weren't for an external cause—God—the universe would not exist at all. God "explains" the universe. But what explains God? God explains God. God explains everything—even God.

So why does something exist rather than nothing? On this view, the universe exists because God created it and God exists because God exists necessarily.

This religious answer is not the only answer to the question of why something exists rather than nothing. Science has several answers—some old, some new. The oldest scientific answer is as old as the oldest religious answer. It says that the reason the universe exists is that the universe has always existed. The universe is infinitely old.

This, however, does not answer our question. This answer didn't work for religion, and it doesn't work for science either. *That* the universe has always existed doesn't explain *why* the universe has always existed.

Could science explain why the universe has always existed? Classical physicists claimed that matter can neither be created nor destroyed. Because the universe exists now, they argued, it must have existed always. Thus something exists because something—in this case the whole universe—exists necessarily.

Is this a better answer than the religious answer? Yes. Everyone agrees that the universe exists. We can see much of it. That God exists is both questionable and controversial. Few of us claim to have seen God. So if we must say that something exists necessarily in order to explain why the universe exists rather than nothing, why not just say that what exists necessarily is the universe itself? What's simpler—the idea of a necessarily existent universe or the idea of a universe *plus* a necessarily existent spiritual being?

One of the most startling scientific developments of all time is the recent theory that the universe has not always existed. In other words, the universe is *not* infinitely old. The latest evidence suggests that the universe had a definite beginning—at least fifteen billion years ago.

In the beginning was the Big Bang. Our universe exploded into existence as an infinitesimally small point and began expanding at the speed of light. Everything—not just the matter that makes up you and us and all the people and objects that have ever existed, but all the matter of every planet and every star in the billions of galaxies—fit into a tiny space smaller than a thimble. There was very little empty space then. But there was the same amount of stuff there is now—it just wasn't as dispersed. Can this amazing Big Bang theory explain why something exists rather than nothing?

No. The Big Bang theory tells us "where" the universe came from—from an infinitesimally small point. But the Big Bang theory doesn't tell us *why* the Big Bang—it doesn't explain the Big Bang. Thus the Big Bang theory doesn't explain why something—in this case the universe—exists rather than nothing.

Perhaps if we knew why the Big Bang, we would know why something exists rather than nothing. So why the Big Bang? One theory is that the Big Bang happened as a result of a previous universe collapsing into the Big Crunch. The momentum from the Big Crunch produced our Big Bang. When our universe runs its course, it will also collapse into another big crunch, which will in turn produce the next big bang and thus the next universe, and so on.

Suppose that this theory of cyclical universes is true. Would it answer our question?

No. The cyclical universe theory merely postpones the question. The birth of our universe is explained by the death of a previous universe, the birth of which is in turn explained by the death of another universe, and so on. This is a bit like paying your American Express bill with another credit card, and then paying the second bill with a third credit card, and so on. You merely postpone paying your bill. If you actually tried this, you'd get arrested for fraud.

But what if you had an infinite number of credit cards? Then you might be able to prolong the billing process forever. Isn't the cyclical universe theory a little like having an infinite number of credit cards? If you had an infinite number of credit cards, you could charge any particular bill. But you'd never actually pay up. You'd merely prolong the billing process—forever. Similarly, the cyclical universe theory could account for the existence of this or any particular universe. But it never answers the question of why something—in this case the whole chain of cyclical universes—exists rather than nothing. It merely prolongs the questioning process forever.

Is this as far as science can go? Suppose the cyclical universe theory is wrong; suppose there *was* a first moment. Then the Big Bang was the moment of creation. Creation has traditionally been considered a religious issue, forever beyond the realm of science. Surprisingly enough, however, some contemporary scientists have ventured even beyond the first moment of creation, beyond the Big Bang. To them, the idea that nothing preceded our universe is not so much a problem as a solution. Neither the Big Crunch nor anything else created our universe. Rather, our universe was created literally from nothing.

Genesis, then, goes like this: In the beginning was nothingness. No God. No space. No time. No matter. No energy. Then the Big Bang: Time, space, and energy exploded into existence out of nowhere and the universe was born.

But how can this "creation of the universe from nothing" scenario explain why something exists rather than nothing? One explanation is that the universe exists because nothingness is unstable. Why the Big Bang? Why something rather than nothing? Because nothingness is unstable. As one physicist recently remarked, "They say there's no such thing as a free lunch. The universe, however, is a free lunch."

An unstable nothingness? It sounds as if "nothingness" is a sort of thing—a mysterious energy-free, space-free, time-free, matter-free object that happened to be unstable. But nothingness is *not* a thing. Nothingness is just nothing.

Here is the way that the "creation of the universe from nothing" scenario tries to explain why something exists rather than nothing: Something—in this case the universe—exists because nothingness, being unstable, degenerated into something. As one philosopher recently put it, nothingness "nothings itself." This answer, however, raises yet another question: Why is nothingness unstable, rather than stable? For if nothingness were stable, there would still be just nothing.

Perhaps there is no reason why nothingness is unstable. Ultimately, then, we could not explain fully why something exists rather than nothing. We would merely have pushed the mystery of existence one step further back.

But perhaps nothingness is unstable for a reason. What could this reason be? It couldn't be that anything *makes* nothingness unstable. There is nothing to make nothingness unstable! So if nothingness is unstable for a reason, it must be that nothingness is unstable by its very nature.

Would this explain why something exists rather than nothing? It might. Two problems remain, however. First, how could nothingness have a nature? If nothingness has a nature, aren't we mislabeling it when we call it *nothingness?* Isn't it then something? And if nothingness is something, then we've merely pushed our question one step further back. We haven't explained why something exists rather than nothing.

Second, why does nothingness have the nature it has rather than some other nature? If there is no reason why nothingness has the nature it has, then the theory can't fully explain why something exists rather than nothing. This theory—that the universe exists because nothingness is unstable by its very nature—would explain why something (in this case, the universe) exists only if there was some reason why nothingness has the nature it has.

There is only one way to explain why nothingness has the nature it has. Since nothingness is just nothing, the explanation would have to be that nothingness itself explains its own instability. There's nothing else to explain it.

But how could nothingness explain its own instability? If nothingness *just happens* to be unstable, it can't. If, on the other hand, nothingness *has* to be unstable, nothingness could explain its own instability. The explanation would be this: Nothingness is unstable because nothingness is *necessarily* unstable.

Suppose then that nothingness is unstable necessarily. It would follow that something exists necessarily. Then something exists rather than nothing because there *has* to be something. But why *this* something? Why a universe? More importantly, why *this* universe rather than, say, a chaotic universe without any life forms? Either there is no explanation of why this universe exists, or else nothingness produced this universe necessarily.

How could nothingness produce the very universe that exists right now—our universe—necessarily? One possibility is based on the idea that we—the questioners—can exist only in a well-ordered universe such as the one that exists right now.

When nothingness degenerates into chaotic universes, we're not there to ask about it. That's why the universe in question—our universe—has to be well ordered. Any universe with questioners in it will be well ordered because that is a requirement for there being any questioners.

Is this so-called Anthropic Principle a good explanation? One problem is that it requires the idea that what comes later can explain what came earlier. Physicists have indeed shown how reverse causation can work in some cases. But whether our presence in the universe can explain why this universe exists remains to be seen. The problem is that the *most* our presence in the universe could explain is the existence of *some* well-ordered universe—one sufficiently ordered and stable to produce questioners. It couldn't explain why *this* universe exists rather than some other, comparably well-ordered universe. Is there any way that the idea of an unstable nothingness could explain the existence of *this* universe?

Yes. The explanation of *this* universe coming into being from nothingness must be that nothingness generated this universe necessarily. In other words, the ultimate explanation of why something exists rather than nothing—if there is an ultimate explanation—must be that this universe exists necessarily.

Suppose, for example, that nothingness did not generate this universe necessarily. Then what could explain this universe? There would be no explanation. So if there is an explanation, it must be that nothingness generated this universe necessarily. Ultimately, then, on this view, *this* universe *must* exist. *This* universe exists necessarily.

Many philosophers past and present think that the question of why something exists rather than nothing is unscientific. Some have claimed that the question is meaningless because it could never, even in principle, be answered. Others have claimed that the question lies in the realm of metaphysics, forever beyond the reach of science.

Science has proven these philosophers wrong. Modern science has not ignored the question of why something exists rather than nothing. For the first time ever, the question has a possible scientific answer based on the idea that because nothingness is necessarily unstable, the universe necessarily exists. Why is there something rather than nothing? Ultimately, because something—the universe—necessarily exists.

Sound familiar? It should. The scientific answer is remarkably like the religious answer. Why does something exist rather than nothing? Because something exists necessarily. For religion, God exists necessarily. For science, the universe exists necessarily.

Science and religion both offer a choice. Either there is no reason why something exists rather than nothing, or else something—either God or the universe—exists necessarily. According to religion, God gives rise to the universe. According to modern science, nothingness gives rise to the universe. According to religion, God gives rise to space and time and matter and energy. According to modern science, nothingness gives rise to space and time and matter and energy.

Isn't it odd that what religion understands by *God* is very close to what modern science understands by *nothingness*? Neither God nor nothingness exists in space or time; both give rise to the universe of space, time, energy, and matter.

What then is the difference between God and nothingness? One difference is that whereas God is essentially stable, nothingness is essentially unstable. This seemingly important difference between God and nothingness masks a genuinely important similarity. Neither God nor nothingness rests content with itself as it is (or is not). God does not just stay God; God gives rise to something. Nothingness does not just stay nothing; it gives rise to something. Both God and nothingness give rise to the *same* something—this universe.

Not remaining the same. Not resting content. Do we have a name for this condition? Theologians call it God. Scientists call it nothingness. If we didn't know better, we'd call it *craving*.

CHAPTER 10

DEATH

When you die you won't vanish into nothing. In one form or another, every bit of material of every person who has ever lived still exists. The same will be true of you. The atoms of your body won't vanish. They will be absorbed by soil, plants, animals, and people.

Every living thing feeds on death. We humans feed on animals and plants. Animals feed either on other animals or on plants. Plants feed on the soil. But all animals and plants, when they die, return to the soil. Death nourishes the soil. Life recycles itself through death.

So, in a sense, of course you will continue to exist after your bodily death. But this is little consolation. You want *you*—not the atoms of your body, but *you*—to survive the decomposition of your body.

If you survive the decomposition of your present physical body, you must survive as something other than your present body—perhaps a soul. But what is a soul, and do you have one? We may not be able to agree on what souls are, but we can agree on what souls are *not*. Souls are not bodies or memories or beliefs or character traits or temperamental dispositions. If souls were bodies, they would decompose when we die. If souls were memories, they would diminish as we got older. If souls were beliefs, they would change from day to day. If souls were character traits or temperamental dispositions, a lobotomy could destroy them.

Traditionally, souls are thought of as "spiritual" substances that *have* memories, beliefs, character traits, and so on; souls are not these phenomena themselves, but, rather, spiritual things that *have* them. Today we know that it is the

body—more specifically, the brain—that has memories, beliefs, character traits, and so on. We can explain the functioning of the body by appeal, ultimately, to the behavior of
atoms.

People used to appeal to souls to explain the functioning of
the body because they thought a spiritual substance was
needed to animate matter. Today we understand matter to be
energy, a universal physical substance—"mass-energy"—that
can account fully, without appeal to souls, for all the properties of living things.

Contemporary psychology has shown us that memories and
beliefs and character traits grow out of experience. Biology
has shown us that bodies, and even some temperamental dispositions, grow out of genes. Physics has shown why atoms
form the sorts of structures that give rise to biology and
psychology. What, then, is left for a soul to do? Apparently
nothing—at least not while the body is alive. After the body
dies, however, the soul supposedly takes over the job
previously done by physical atoms. Souls, then, in a sense, are
spiritual atoms. It takes only one soul—one spiritual atom—to
do the job of lots of material atoms.

Souls and physical atoms are both invisible to the naked
eye. However, whereas physical atoms are visible through
electron microscopes, souls are not visible at all. It is not just
that we need better microscopes to see souls. Even if we had
devices through which we saw colors or shapes surrounding
bodies, we'd be looking at colors and shapes, which are
physical phenomena, not souls. We could *never* see souls, even
in principle, through any physical device, because souls are
not physical phenomena.

Are souls a possible answer to whether there is life after
death? Perhaps. But they are a redundant answer. Bodies are
composed of atoms. Souls are a kind of spiritual atom. If you
were dissatisfied with the answer that you survive your bodily death because the atoms of your body survive, then why be
satisfied with the answer that you survive because your
spiritual atom survives? Billions of nearly indestructible but
verifiable physical atoms from your body survive your bodily
death and you are dissatisfied. One spiritual atom—which

could never, even in principle, be observed—survives, and you are satisfied. Why?

Isn't it because you think that physical atoms could not possibly sustain your psychology after the death of your physical body, whereas your spiritual atom could? But why assume this? Perhaps your physical atoms, even as dispersed as they would be after death, could sustain your psychology. There is no evidence that they could; but it is *possible* that they could. Which is more bizarre—the idea that your psychology is somehow preserved by physical atoms, which are known to exist, or that your psychology is somehow preserved by a nonphysical, spiritual atom, which is not known to exist and which cannot even in principle be observed?

Perhaps we have gone too fast. Perhaps there is evidence that souls exist. After all, isn't there evidence that some people have survived their bodily deaths?

Right now we are not questioning whether there is evidence that some people have survived their bodily deaths. Even if there were such evidence, our point is simply that there is no reason to believe that souls have anything to do with it because there is no evidence that souls exist. More than that, there *couldn't* be any evidence that souls exist. Yet—surprisingly enough—there still might be evidence that some people have survived their bodily deaths.

So let us turn to the question of whether there is any evidence that some people have survived their bodily deaths. After all, what difference does it make if you survive your bodily death as a soul or if you survive in some physical way? The mode of transportation is a mere detail. Survival, on the other hand, is a matter of life and death.

Everyone has heard stories about life after death. There are the old-fashioned religious stories. There are the new-fashioned psychic phenomena stories. Is there any truth to any of them?

The religious stories may or may not be true. But this much is certain: If we are to accept religious stories as evidence, we will end up with contradictory evidence. There are many different religious stories from many different religious traditions, and these stories contradict each other. Some say that after death we immediately continue existing in another world. Others say that after death we cease to exist until the final day of this world. Some say we leave Earth forever and go to either a heaven or a hell. Still others say we are reborn on Earth again and again and again. Some say we survive as material beings. Others say we survive as spiritual beings. Some say we survive as personal beings, whereas others say that, eventually, we lose our individuality completely and merge with the cosmos. Some say we spend eternity sitting at the feet of God. Others say we are God. We could go on for another twenty pages or so, but our point should be obvious: Religious stories cancel each other out. Perhaps that's why, throughout history, religious *people* have tried to cancel each other out!

One of these religious stories, however, may still be true. Even if one of these stories is true, none of them is *evidence* that anyone has ever survived bodily death. For every story there is another equally credible story that contradicts it, and contradictory evidence is self-defeating evidence—it is like having no evidence at all. If there is evidence for life after death, it must be found elsewhere.

But couldn't someone argue that, *collectively*, the religious stories provide good evidence for life after death? After all, the diverse religious stories do agree on one thing: survival. They differ merely on the details. So aren't they good evidence for survival? No. Agreement in this case merely shows that a common theme can be found in almost all the world's religions. Psychology can easily explain this common theme. One psychology text puts it like this: "Stimuli pertaining to death can be regarded as a subset of the larger set of stimuli that elicit avoidance or distress responses." In other words: People fear death. Not just here and there, or once in a while, but everywhere and always. Fearing death, people have a strong motive to deny it.

Someone might not agree with this explanation of why religious stories tend to promote the idea of survival of bodily death. Someone might think that the religious stories suggest a truth about survival, not a truth about human psychology. But the explanation in terms of human psychology is not only simpler, it is testable. The explanation in terms of survival, on the other hand, is speculative at best, more complex, and impossible to test either directly or indirectly. Thus believing in survival on the basis of religious stories isn't belief based on good evidence. It is belief based on faith. Not *just* on faith, but on faith that goes *contrary* to the best available evidence.

So much for the old-fashioned religious stories. What about the new-fashioned psychic phenomena stories? These stories vary a lot in specifics, but they can all be broadly categorized in terms of the three basic types of phenomena they describe: remembrances of past lives, apparitions of dead people, and experiences of dying and coming back. Because each type of phenomenon includes many subcategories, the result may seem a bewildering array of different sorts of arguments. There is, however, a simple common core to all arguments based on such evidence. They can all be understood as having two premises and a conclusion. The first premise is that some unusual phenomenon has happened—an apparition, a memory of a past life, a strange experience, and so on. The second (usually implicit) premise is that *the best explanation* of the unusual phenomenon implies that someone has survived bodily death. The conclusion is that someone *has* survived bodily death.

There is never just one possible explanation of the report of the unusual phenomenon, but four: (1) fraud, (2) unknown but ordinary circumstances, (3) some psychic phenomenon like ESP, and (4) survival of bodily death. For instance, if someone under hypnosis claims to remember doing things he or she did in some previous life, it might be a trick—fraud. Or the person might be apparently remembering information learned in some ordinary—but forgotten—way. Or the person might have ESP—that is, he or she might not be remembering a previous life but picking up the information in some other extraordinary (but eventually explicable) way. Or the person might actually be remembering a previous life. These four possibilities have to be weighed against each other. For the evidence to show that people survive their bodily deaths, the evidence must favor the survival hypothesis—the fourth possible explanation—more than the other three.

People who consider reports of such unusual phenomena are often unaware that there are four possible explanations. They frequently assume there is just one explanation—survival. Furthermore, they are often unaware that to make the case, on the basis of evidence, that the particular explanation they favor is the most probable one, they must *show* that their favorite explanation is better supported by evidence than are the other three. Therefore, given these four possible explanations of any unusual phenomenon, do such phenomena provide adequate evidence for survival of bodily death? To provide such evidence, the survival hypothesis would at least sometimes have to be the most likely explanation. Is it ever?

To decide, we must remember to consider all relevant information, such as, for instance, that the person relating the incident often stands to gain something—money, prestige, credibility—and thus often has a motive for fraudulent behavior. If the person does have a motive for fraudulent behavior, this doesn't prove that the person is a fraud. But it counts in favor of the fraud explanation and against the other three possible explanations. Thus, in the end, we have to ask ourselves which is the more plausible explanation: that the person is pulling a clever trick or that someone has actually survived bodily death.

Suppose, however, that you have information that counts against fraud; for instance, the person apparently remembering a previous life is *you*. In that case, is survival of bodily death the most plausible explanation?

Not necessarily. The survival hypothesis still has to be weighed against the other two explanations. One possibility is that your memory was stimulated by some information you acquired in a normal way. For instance, you read as a child about a place you've never been to and now you think you remember having actually been there. Which is more plausible—that some such unusual turn of events resulted in your making a mistake, or that you are actually remembering a previous life? The same applies to the additional possibility of self-deception. What could be the motive for self-deception? Fear could, or the desire to reduce anxiety about death.

The obvious first step is to do more checking. There is

always the chance that the phenomenon in question, no matter how "strange," will have an ordinary explanation. There is also the chance it won't. To support the survival hypothesis, however, it is not enough that *at present* there is no known explanation of the phenomenon. The chance that there is some as yet unknown, but ordinary, explanation must be weighed against the likelihood of the survival explanation. Thus, barring further information, in the case we've been considering, which is the *likelier* explanation: that your apparent remembering of a previous life has some ordinary explanation, or that you actually remember your previous life?

Suppose further information makes it unlikely that there is an ordinary explanation of your apparent remembering. Suppose, for instance, that you are a four-year-old who has just identified a perfect "stranger" as the man who murderered you *ten years ago*. Furthermore, you give his name, the location of the murder, and you relate evidence that, when checked, is found to be true and is sufficient to convict him. You seem to remember all the details as if they happened to you. Would this be adequate to show that you actually survived your bodily death?

No. The survival hypothesis has now to be weighed against the ESP explanation. For the survival hypothesis to win, however, there must be more evidence for it than for the ESP explanation. This, ultimately, is where the survival hypothesis always faces its most severe challenge.

There might someday be evidence that survival of bodily death is a more likely explanation of the new-fashioned psychic phenomena stories than is the ESP explanation. But it is hard to see how that could be the case today. Even if we assume that ESP actually exists, we have almost no idea how it works. Thus we have little reason for concluding that ESP could *not* produce the unusual phenomena. Out-of-body experiences, near-death experiences, apparitions, and so on, are— today at least—as well explained by ESP as they are by the survival hypothesis.

This is not to say that the ESP explanation is necessarily better than the survival hypothesis, or that either is necessarily better than one of the first two alternatives. Our point is that it is difficult to make the case that the evidence that now exists favors the survival hypothesis over *all other* possible explanations. And that is what the survival hypothesis would have to do to emerge as the most likely explanation. Thus no evidence that now exists from new-fashioned psychic phenomena stories provides good evidence for believing that people survive their bodily deaths.

So much for both the new-fashioned psychic phenomena stories and the old-fashioned religious stories. Where does this leave us?

It leaves us where we began: with life *before* death. If you find this depressing, recall that the parts out of which you are composed, both physical and mental, are constantly "dying" and being replaced. In a sense, our ordinary, day-to-day lives, *are* a kind of life after death!

So we do, after all, get life after death. We get it where we never expected it. *Here.*

CHAPTER 11

MEANING

Why are we here? What's it all about? Is there some purpose or meaning to life?

At one time or another, everyone asks such questions. As children and as old people, especially, we wonder: Why? What does it all mean? Most of the rest of the time, we're so busy trying to be successful we don't worry about meaning. But even then, in the back of our minds, we may still wonder. And when we do, what is it we really want to know?

Suppose you're at a party. You love being with the people there; they love having you there. The music is terrific, the food and drinks are delicious, and everything is paid for. No one has to go anywhere, do anything, be any particular way. Everyone is having a wonderful time. Suddenly someone turns to you and asks, "Why are we here? What is the meaning of this party?" You'd probably consider the question irrelevant. Suppose, on the other hand, the party is terrible. Then you might think the question has a point.

So also with the question "What is the meaning of life?" When life is wonderful, we don't ask what it means—we're too busy enjoying it. When life is a painful struggle, the question forces itself upon us not so much because we want to answer the question of the meaning of life but, rather, because we want to end our struggle. We don't then care about solving the problem of the *meaning* of life. We care about solving the problem of *life*.

Everyone wants to have a good time. And it seems everyone has a recipe. Yet nearly everyone is struggling. There must be something wrong with the recipes.

Nearly everyone *is* struggling, not only in the poorest parts

of the world, but everywhere. Poor people struggle just to survive, but even affluent people struggle. Everywhere, nearly everyone is *always* struggling. Why? What can we do about our
struggles? Isn't that what we usually want to know, when the
question of the meaning of life bothers us?

Theoretical answers may be of theoretical interest. But
even after all the philosophy books, novels, songs, poems, and
movies, people are still struggling. Lots of answers to the
meaning of life have been given—some serious, some funny,
some clever, some stupid—but none of them have ended the
struggle. Why?

The problem is not that we don't have enough answers to
the question, "What is the meaning of life?" (we have too
many) but that our lives are a struggle. It's not necessarily
that the answers are wrong (though since most of them are
incompatible with each other most of them must be wrong) but
that the answers don't end the struggle. Why is that?

The problem is with the answers. And there are two
problems. The first problem is that almost all the answers are
answers to the wrong question. They attempt to tell us the
meaning of life when what we need is a solution to life's
struggles.

Second, the problem with the answers is *that they are answers*. For even if we had the answer to the question of why
life is such a struggle, this would not by itself end life's
struggles. Knowing *why* life is such a struggle might change
things a great deal. But answers can't be the answer. To see
why, we shall first have to answer the question of why life is
a struggle, since until we have that answer, it will always be
tempting to suppose that if only we did have the answer, it
would end life's struggles.

So why is life such a struggle? What's the answer?

Everyone knows it takes two to have a fight. You can't be
involved in a struggle unless someone or something is resisting.
The resistance may come from the outside or from the inside—
either you are divided from someone else, or from your
environment, or from yourself. Without division there can be
no resistance. Without resistance there can be no struggle.

So the way to stop struggling is to end the fragmentation

that leads to resistance. The problem is that we don't want to stop struggling at the cost of being dominated. If we drop all resistance, someone else is sure to dominate us. But even people whom no one is trying to dominate, even those in control, are struggling. In some places in the world, and at some times, struggle comes from the outside. But at all places in the world, and at all times, struggle comes from the inside.

What is *your* internal struggle? You're reading this book. Chances are no one is trying to shoot you. Chances are, though, that you are bothered by some internal struggle. How can you live without internal struggle? When you're bothered by questions about the meaning of life, isn't that what you usually want to know?

External and internal struggle both can be stopped in the same way: Drop all resistance. The problem with this answer in the case of external struggle is that we're afraid of being dominated. But no such problem exists in the case of internal struggle. In fact, just the opposite is the case. The reason you're bothered by internal struggle in the first place is that you're trying to dominate yourself—one part of you is trying to dominate another part of you.

Consider the simplest possible example of internal struggle. Suppose you drink too much alcohol and it bothers you. Part of you wants to continue. Another part of you wants to quit. If *all* of you wants to continue drinking, there is no struggle, you just drink. If *all* of you wants to quit, there is no struggle, you just quit. The problem is how to decide which part of yourself should prevail—in this case, the drinker or the nondrinker—and then how to get the other part to stop resisting.

Almost all internal struggle follows the same pattern. There is what you *are* and there is what you think you *should* be. That is the essence of internal conflict. (That's why many of the answers to the meaning of life, such as religious answers, merely fuel the problem of internal struggle: they widen the gap by distancing you from yourself, that is, by creating within you an idealization of you.) So, which part should prevail—the actual you, who exists right now, or the ideal you, who might exist sometime in the future?

You might end your internal struggle in two ways: by eventually becoming the ideal you, or by accepting yourself exactly as you are right now and dropping all notions of how you should be. The first way, you continue struggling with yourself in the hope your struggle will end some day. The second way, you stop struggling right away.

It is difficult to drop being the way we are. It is easier to drop all notions of how we should be. We might eventually be able to change the way we are, but "trying to change" is a sure formula for perpetuating the struggle.

So, in the simple case of the drinker versus the nondrinker, who wins? For the time being, the drinker wins. That doesn't necessarily mean that the drinker will *always* be a drinker. Maybe—but not necessarily. Accepting the fact of being a drinker, accepting it without condition that you change, may, as we shall see, be an effective way to become a nondrinker. The evolution might not take place, but there is a *chance* it will. One thing is certain: If the evolution does take place, it will be effortless.

But what if the drinker is addicted? Won't surrendering all resistance mean oblivion and death? Perhaps. But continuing to struggle with addiction might also mean oblivion and death—after great effort and pain! If one must drink oneself to death, isn't it better to do it effortlessly, rather than with great struggle and pain?

We are all addicted to one thing or another. Accepting ourselves as we are without the condition that we change might give us insight into the causes of our addictions. For instance, one major reason people enjoy alcohol is that it makes them less inhibited. But why are they inhibited in the first place? Isn't that kind of inhibition often the result of their own resistance against what they themselves really are? Alcohol takes away inhibition and allows the inhibited part to come out. Often, self-destructive behavior is the inhibited part of you, ordinarily repressed by the ideal you, finally exerting itself and saying, "If you don't let me out, I'll kill you!" So the drinker who allows self-acceptance might become less inhibited—even without alcohol—and, in turn, might be less prone to drug abuse.

But if we all cease struggling, won't we just lie around all day? What will move us to act? Perhaps nothing. We might lie around all day. But one thing that *could* move us to act is love of some activity. We don't need to be coerced into doing what we love to do.

So whatever your struggle, the way out of that struggle might be to accept yourself as you are without the condition that you change. The alternative would be to keep struggling. That's the alternative most of us take because, deep down, we believe that struggle is the price we must pay for success. Without struggle, we think, we could never go from being what we are now to being the successful person we would someday like to be. But there is something suspicious about this strategy: Nearly everyone is struggling, yet few are successful.

Ordinarily, when we call someone successful, we're talking about career. That is only one kind of success. You can also be successful as a person—for instance, by being happy and by contributing to the happiness of others. Professional and personal success don't necessarily go together. We all know people who are successful in their careers but failures as persons and many people who have failed in their careers but are successful as persons. Struggling does not ensure either kind of success. Does anything?

There may be no single key to having a successful career. But there is a common element: The farmer who becomes a successful farmer, the doctor who becomes a successful doctor, the playwright who becomes a successful playwright, and so on, all become successful by pleasing others. To make money, for instance, you have to sell something or provide a service that someone else wants to pay for. Somewhere down the line, all types of professional success require pleasing others.

What, then, of being successful as a person? Oddly enough, here too success usually requires pleasing others. Being happy at work, being a good friend, a good parent, a good lover, and so on, all ultimately involve pleasing others.

Few of us are hermits. Even pleasing ourselves usually involves pleasing others. We may like to think of ourselves as individualists. The truth is that being successful as a person—being happy and contributing to the happiness of others—almost always involves pleasing others. So a common element to both professional and personal success is pleasing others.

Instinctively we already know this. But we tend to view ourselves through the lens of an idealized self-image that exaggerates the extent of our independence. We don't like to admit the extent to which we depend, even for our happiness, on the approval of others. We like to think that we don't care what people think of us. The truth is, we do care. This creates a tension within us, an internal struggle between the part of us that wants approval and the part that wants independence from the need for approval.

There is an ironic twist to this tension within us. We think the way to independence is through success. But the way to success is almost always through the approval of others. The student, the architect, the actor, the grocer, the football player, are all dependent on the approval of bosses, clients, fans, and so on, to gain greater independence from their need for approval.

We're all in the same boat. For instance, the authors of this book think that if this book is a great success, they will become more independent and will be better able to go where they want, do what they want, write what they want, and so on, without having to worry about what others think. The authors want to free themselves from the need for approval. How are they going to do it? Like everyone else, they will gain their independence from the need for the approval of others by gaining the approval of others. How smart!

This irony about success cuts deeply into all of our lives. Consider, for example, the way power is distributed in a romantic relationship. The one who is more powerful is the one who is less dependent on the other. How do you get less dependent? Usually by having more choice as to who you are with. The better you are at pleasing others, all else being equal, the more choice you have as to who you are with. The more choice you have, the more independent you are. So even in romantic relationships the way to independence is through pleasing others. Ironically, the way to independence is through dependence.

Such are society's mechanisms for keeping us in line.

Without our need to seek the approval of others, society would collapse. The very structure of society—no matter what the society's particular mores are—depends on social cohesion. One way society ensures this cohesion is by linking our need to be independent with our need for approval. Society breeds the desire for independence into us to ensure that, as individuals, we will be dependent on the approval of others, thereby ensuring social cohesion. We depend on approval because only through approval can we hope to achieve independence. Our desire for independence is part of the very glue of social cohesion.

It may seem, then, from what we've just said, that seeking approval is the key to success. If success is impossible without approval, then the way to success would seem to be to aim directly for it. That is what most of us do.

This strategy can't be completely wrong. After all, we've just seen that the approval of others is necessary for success. For instance, most students want to get good grades. That is their criterion of success. Students instinctively know that the surest way to get good grades is to get approval from their teachers by agreeing with them. This strategy works—but only to a point. It often, but not always, ensures that the student gets good grades. But merely getting good grades is a mediocre level of success. As every good teacher knows, those students who reach a high level of success in school—academic excellence—develop the capacity for *independent* thought. Getting good grades, on the other hand, usually doesn't ensure that a student has developed this capacity.

Students who agree with their teachers tend to get good grades partly because imitating their teachers' views on the material they are studying is the first level of connecting to that material. The best students then go on to challenge the opinions of their teachers in creative ways. The best students, once they have achieved the initial connection between themselves and the subject matter through imitating the teacher, then go on to connect to the subject matter directly. This requires taking risks—in particular, risking the disapproval of their teachers. Ultimately, what must matter most to these students is not the connection between themselves and their teachers, but the connection between themselves and their subject matter.

Seeking approval is the first step to success. But it only goes so far. In the end, it is even limiting. If you want to reach the higher levels of success, you must win approval not by seeking it but rather by achieving some level of excellence through connecting directly to the activity you are involved in. The twist is that such a level of excellence through direct connecting to an activity can never be attained so long as one is primarily concerned with seeking approval. To attain success in its fullest form one must drop the quest for approval.

People tend to think success has something to do with pleasing others because that is itself an indirect way of connecting with an activity. But pleasing others is also a by-product of connecting directly with an activity. In the end, what matters most is not approval but connecting directly with an activity, for that is the way to attain a high level of success. For instance, you might get a promotion by pleasing your boss, a job as an actor by pleasing a director, a lucrative business contract by pleasing a client, and so on. All these initial successes are like the student getting a good grade by pleasing the teacher. Whether you are successful in your new job once you have it, whether you are successful as an actor, grocer, teacher, or whatever, will ultimately depend on how you connect to whatever activity your job requires.

What does it mean to connect directly to an activity? First, consider professional success. The purpose of all professions is to make a product. For instance, doctors cultivate health, architects design buildings, playwrights write plays, and so on. Many people view their work-related activities merely as instruments for producing products. They don't value the process that leads to the product as an end in itself. The ones who do, however, are the ones who become most successful. The student who loves to study, the boxer who loves to box, the runner who loves to run, the farmer who loves to farm, all experience the same joy of activity. They love the *process*, not just the product, and so they succeed to a much greater degree.

Suppose you repair bicycles. Fixing bicycles is the process.

A fixed bicycle is the product. You want to be a successful bicycle repairman. How? You can't be successful unless you please your clients. You must turn damaged or faulty bicycles into good ones, and you must do it efficiently and well. You can do this at a minimal level if you merely want to please your customers. You can do it much better if you love to repair bicycles.

But every activity, every process, it would seem, has its drudgery. In bicycle repair, you have to repack the ball bearings, grease the chains, adjust the cables. Ordinarily, such chores are drudgery because, as we do them, we focus on getting them done instead of on doing them. When we focus on getting them done we are not all there. Our hands are there and perhaps part of our minds are there, but another part of us constantly projects into the future. If we are completely there, focused on our activity, paying attention to everything we do, our activity, no matter what it is, will rarely be drudgery. Almost always, our desire to get it over with makes it drudgery.

Suppose, for instance, you are told to set up and then dismantle a toy city. It will take hours of patient, detailed work to set up the city, only to destroy it in the end. How would you react? As you were doing it, you'd probably be thinking: What is the purpose of this? I want to finish, get some sleep before I have to go to work, and so on.

Yet when we were children, we played like that for hours on end. Did we worry then about the purpose of building toy cities, only to dismantle them as soon as we finished? What was the purpose of building them? Wasn't it simply the act of doing it? When we were children, we played games not to be done with them, but to do them. That's why we enjoyed them so much. Isn't that the very source of the magic of childhood?

Living is a series of activities that involves everything you do, including your job. Living is your activity. The product is *you*. Being connected to your life means, ultimately, being connected to all the activities of your life. These activities continually produce new versions of you. Being connected means valuing these activities not merely as a means to an end—as a means to producing a certain type of you—but rather as ends in themselves.

Consider, for example, the activity of keeping yourself physically fit. It can be done primarily as an end in itself. Or it can be done as a mere means to fitness. Ask yourself this: Who will be more physically fit after five years—the person who flogs himself into jogging every morning, or the person who so enjoys the physical act of running that she does it willingly every day?

If in all your activities the thing you focus on is the finished product—the read book, the fixed bicycle, the delivered mail, the college degree, the ideal you—happiness will elude you. Happiness might surface after you have completed something, but then it is usually time to start something else. Then you rush through the next project, struggling with yourself because you don't really want to be doing it either. You just want to have done it, to be finished.

If you are connected to the process, the main reward isn't with the finishing. It's with the doing. The finishing may even have a sorrowful aspect to it because it will signify the end of a particular process. For the authors of this book, for instance, when the last word is written, when the final revision is sent off to the publisher, there will be joy. There will also be sorrow because a process they love will have ended. There might be other books, other processes. But *this* particular process will have ended forever.

So also with the process of being a person. When a life that has been good is nearing completion, there will be sorrow. There might also be the joy of completion. There might even be other lives. But *this* life, *this* particular process, will have ended forever.

The key to success in life, then, is connecting, not with a product, but with a process: ultimately, with the process of being yourself. Where there is genuine connection to a process, there will be success.

Success makes our lives rich and full of meaning. And where there is success, there will ultimately also be sorrow because it is the nature of all processes to change, and by changing they end.

What, then, about the meaning of life?

The many answers that have been given, as we have

suggested, are answers to the wrong question. They attempt to tell us the meaning of life when what we need is a solution to life's struggles. The real question is, "Why is life such a struggle?"

We have an answer: Life is a struggle because we are divided against each other and also against ourselves. But do we have a solution to life's struggles? No. We remain divided. We remain struggling. Why?

Looking for answers is looking in the wrong place. Answers are not the answer. What we need is what none who live attached to answers have: wisdom.

CHAPTER 12

ETHICS

From childhood on you are told not just who you are and what the world is, but what to do and how to do it, what to think and how to think it, how to talk and whom to talk to, what to say and when to say it, what not to say and when not to say it, whom to listen to and whom not to, what matters most and what matters least, what's proper and what isn't, what is right and what is wrong, which goals to seek and which not to, when to have sex and when not to and with whom and why; good words, bad words, good music, bad music, good books, bad books, good people, bad people; how to dress, how to walk, how to eat, whom to trust, how to behave, how to treat others, how to treat yourself, how to become secure, rich, successful, happy—the list is endless. The advice is endless. And it will continue until you die.

Parents, teachers, lawmakers, politicians, and religious leaders are trying to train you how to fit into the world they inherited from their parents, teachers, lawmakers, politicians and religious leaders, who in turn inherited it from their authorities, and so on. Why are they doing this?

Obvious answer: You need to be trained to behave well, think well, live well, and so on, because you are by nature bad. Left to your own devices, you would think the wrong thoughts, say the wrong things, feel the wrong emotions, and behave terribly towards others. Without proper training you would lead yourself and others to ruin. You need social, political, and religious leaders to keep you in line.

But, first, how do the authorities in charge of your conditioning know you are, by nature, bad? Without authorities constantly trying to condition you—trying to get you to believe and behave as they want you to believe and behave—you *might* grow up at least as good as you are now. Perhaps authorities know through experience that all people are, by nature, bad. But how could they know this through experience? When were people ever allowed to discover for themselves, without being prodded by some authority or other, what life is all about and to decide for themselves how best to live?

There has never been a time, in recorded history, when people have not been conditioned by social, political, or religious leaders. So the assumption that without being trained by authorities you would be bad has never been tested. Rather, the assumption has simply been passed down, generation after generation, from one authority to another, without question, perhaps because authorities find it convenient not to question an assumption which entails that they, the authorities, are indispensable—that without them to keep us in line we would all run amok.

Second, if all people are naturally bad, won't the people who become authorities also be bad? The only difference will be that besides being bad, the authorities will be powerful. Unless in the process of being trained or in gaining power over others bad people are reliably transformed into good people, the tradition of authority will generally give rise to a world in which a bunch of bad, powerful people have dominion over a bunch of bad, weak people. Becoming an authority might even make a person worse: "Power corrupts, and absolute power corrupts absolutely."

Third, why do the leaders who have so many answers have so many problems? The same people who are training you how to think and act and feel are trying (so they say) to spare you from problems which (and this they conveniently fail to mention) they have not managed to avoid themselves. Their thoughts are often confused, their actions callous and reprehensible, their lives a painful struggle. If the trainers are giving you what their trainers gave them, then perhaps not only is the training not working, the training may well be the source of the problem.

Fourth, and most importantly, how do social, political and

religious authorities know what's best? Perhaps it's simply a case of "Father knows best." Since the beginning of recorded history, the people in charge have nearly always been males. Males as heads of families, males as heads of state, males as the great philosophers, males as the great writers, males as the great painters, musicians, and inventors, males as originators of religion and, finally, males as God. Perhaps the problem is that the trainers in charge of the training have been males!

That males have been the problem is probably as close to absolute truth as one can get in a relativistic universe. However, when women become leaders they can be as insufferable, dogmatic, power hungry, corrupt, and vicious as the worst of males. Of course, women have had to wrestle power away from men within an already patriarchal society. Perhaps in a society created and controlled by women, women would be better trainers than men have ever been. But the question is not whether women would be better trainers than men. The question is whether we need trainers at all. "Mother knows best" is just a variation of "Father knows best." What reason is there for thinking that *anybody* knows best?

One would certainly think that so many authorities with so many answers would have succeeded in creating societies in which people live wonderful, happy, successful lives. But their track record doesn't exactly take one's breath away (except, perhaps, literally). Maybe there is no alternative to authority and we are stuck. But if whipping a horse won't make it go faster, why beat the poor beast?

Perhaps the authorities know that, in the long run, the method of authority will get you to where you ought to be. But how do they know that? Traditionally, the answer—the grand bulwark of authority—has been "God." *He* passes down truths about how you should live. Your job is to learn God's truths and that takes training. Invariably, however, for some reason God chooses not to pass these truths down to *you* but to *them*, usually to whomever is already in power. Why God would choose to reveal the truth only to some religious and political middle*men* instead of to everybody is perhaps one of those mysterious, wonderous ways God works.

But even if God does hand down truths to a few choice authorities about how you should live, how do you know which authorities are the genuine ones? God doesn't extend a hand from the sky and point them out to you. It is conveniently left to the authorities themselves to enlighten you about who the proper authorities are. Invariably, they point to themselves or to members of their own groups, often disagreeing vehemently among themselves about who the proper authorities are—often to the point of killing each other or (more usually) inspiring their followers to do the killing and dying.

So how do you know which "divinely inspired" truths are the real ones? You could just pick whichever ones your own authorities have taught you and leave it at that. But that would be arbitrary. And, anyway, *why* should you do this? Because your authorities say so? Why should you listen? Because that's what they say is best for you? How do they *know* what is best for you? Because God told them? How do *you* know God told them? Because *they* say so? How do you know the authorities aren't lying or deceived? You don't. So even if some authorities do get their truths from God, it doesn't do you any good. And, simply supposing that they do has led, historically, to intolerance, violence, bloodshed, suffering, repression, confusion, fear, hatred, and death.

Perhaps, though, some authorities get their truths not from God but from reason. If that were the case, that might work for them, but what about you? The first problem, once again, is that even the authorities who claim to rely on reason disagree about what reason dictates. How do you know which secular authorities to trust? If comparably credentialed authorities disagree, then those who are not authorities have no basis for believing one authority rather than another.

In addition, just as you have ample reason to suspect that religious authorities are not genuine authorities on how you should live, so you have ample reason to suspect that secular authorities are not genuine authorities on how you should live. Their performance thus far is hardly inspiring. For instance, secular believers in the power of reason have pleaded and plotted for centuries for a chance to seize the reins of political power from believers in God. Finally, in the twentieth century, they got their chance. Some improvement! Secular political authorities who claim their answers are based not on faith but on reason have been just as ruthless, dogmatic, corrupt, and vicious as their religious counterparts. If secular leaders have succeeded in showing that the authority of reason is greater than the authority of faith, they have also showed that the problem is not with the basis of authority but that authority may well be the basis of the problem.

One problem is that authorities tend to want to preserve their positions of authority, regardless of whether they are in the right or in the wrong, by establishing a set of societal and legal procedures that not only preserve their power but increase it over time. By creating a social structure in which their threats can be carried out, they can make it true that accepting what they *claim* is best for you *is* best for you. If you don't obey, you'll get hurt—*by them*! They can say, as fathers often do, "you'd better listen, if you know what's good for you," not as a way of showing rationally that what they claim is in your best interest really is in your best interest, but as a way of using their position of power to subjugate your will to theirs. But unless the authorities know that whatever you are being ordered to do really is in your best interest (Is it? How do they know?), and unless you know that the authorities have your interests in mind (Do they? How do you know?) rather than their own, obedience to authority does not solve the problem of how best to live. And unless the authorities are on the right track, obedience may lead you further astray and possibly destroy you.

What, then, ought you to do? Perhaps you should ignore external authorities and rely, instead, on the internal authority of your own conscience to tell you what is right and what is wrong, how to behave, what your values should be, and so on.

However, most of the same problems that arose in the case of external authority arise also for conscience. Just as the external authorities disagree, so do the dictates of conscience. Different people have radically different intuitions, feelings, attitudes, and so on, about how best to live. Even any one your conscience is a doorway to the truth, why should you trust even the internal authority of your own conscience?

Our consciences seem to vary too much with culture and conditioning to be doorways to the truth. For instance, most Americans who would be repulsed by the sight of someone cooking and eating a dog have no trouble eating cows. Yet most (Asian) Indians would be more horrified by the sight of someone killing and eating a cow than of someone killing and eating a dog. Such sympathies arise as a result of conditioning by various social, religious, and political authorities. Or, to take another example, a white American male of the early nineteenth century would probably be repulsed by the sight of a black man and a white woman kissing. Even today, inter-racial love affairs give many people bad feelings. Such feelings are merely the result of antiquated traditions, which in turn are the result of conditioning, which in turn is the result of social, religious, and political authorities at work telling you what to think, what to feel, and how to behave, all for your own good. Which leads straight to the possibility that conscience is but external authority internalized.

Familial, societal, religious, and political ideologies have been so ingrained in most of us that they speak to us from within, guiding us with our own feelings. But why then trust your feelings? If morality cannot be based on authority, and if conscience is merely the result of deeply ingrained conditioning—merely external authority internalized—then morality cannot be based on conscience. What reason, then, is there to trust *anybody* for moral guidance—*including yourself*?

But if there is nothing and nobody you can trust for moral guidance, where does that leave you?

CHAPTER 13

VALUES

All your life you've been told to adopt ideals, to see yourself—your family, your nationality, your race, your culture, your world—through the tinted lenses of inherited values. You've been taught to label everything yes or no, good or bad, right or wrong, and to appeal to authorities and, through them, to stick ready-made answers onto everything.

Most people fall into line. Those few who rebel and march to the beat of a different drummer usually still march, following, in their rebellion, a path paved with values not their own but of their peers. Even those who resolve to follow only their own personal consciences follow a conscience that is itself largely the product of elaborate social and cultural conditioning.

Meanwhile, almost everyone is obsessed with two practical questions: What do I want? and How can I get it? Ironically (but not surprisingly, given the external sources of most of our values), when we get what we want, often we no longer want it (and then we can't get rid of it!). Or, if we do still want it, either we can't keep it or else it is not enough; we want more. And if and when we get more, that too is ultimately not satisfying. The result, often, is a frustration that breeds deep cynicism, consoled, if at all, only by the grim realization that it may not matter all that much in the end anyway because (so far as we know) what awaits us in the end is just death, and then worms: Everything and everybody now alive will someday be dead, humanity itself will become extinct, the sun will blow up, the books will burn, the statues will melt, the cities will be annihilated. There will be nothing left, not even Earth; the whole universe will ultimately implode itself out of existence or die a slow heat-death. If nothingness or ashes is the destiny of everything, what it all comes to in the end, what, then, is the value *of* our lives? What should be the values *in* our lives? Is there something meaningful and valuable we can do, or are we just cows stuck on a conveyor belt on the way to the saw?

We can't, it seems, avoid the saw; we can't last forever. Nor can any of the things we create last forever. We can, however, be here fully for the time we do have by making our lives our own. Otherwise, it is as if we never even existed except as placeholders, receptacles for conditioning, or—if we become authorities—conveyor belts for transmitting unexamined answers, like cultural debris, from our conditioners to those we ourselves condition.

By examining our lives, we may be able to wrest ourselves from inherited answers and hand-me-down values long enough to make contact—not with pipe-dreams or idealizations—but with what is true and authentic about ourselves and the world. While we may not, ultimately, save ourselves, we can stand up to the disintegrating universe, our destroyer, and in the midst of our annihilation take stock of what is really going on, before the world hurtles us and then itself into oblivion. But how?

By the time the idea of questioning our values even occurs to us, we have already internalized so many values that if we try to question these values while remaining committed to them, our questioning is likely to be inauthentic, or, at the very least, limited and limiting in that it would entail accepting, without question, many of the very value-assumptions we were trying to question. Perhaps this is the best we can do. But it would be revealing if we could get entirely outside our frameworks of values, beyond their scope, to get a neutral perspective on them (if there even is such a thing as a neutral perspective).

To do so, we would have to let go of our values long enough for them to let go of us. The Christian would have to cease being a Christian, the American would have to cease being an American, the Communist would have to cease being a Communist, and so on—not in the sense of ceasing to be affiliated with whatever religious, national, or political group generates whatever set of values one subscribes to—but in the sense of suspending commitment to these values. We would have to set aside our familial and cultural values and get beyond even our consciences—not necessarily for the purpose of dispensing permanently with these values, or to attach ourselves to some new values, but as an exercise in getting temporarily far enough beyond the scope of our values so that we can at least examine them without presupposing the very values we are examining, or any other values, except for the value of seeing ourselves and the world exactly as we are.

The question, then, is how to unhook your thoughts and feelings from whatever value-anchors now secure and bind you to your present point of view. It's unrealistic to suppose you can simply drop all your values—that is, that you can just stop expressing any of your values to others or even stop thinking them (consciously or unconsciously) to yourself. Your values—your ideas about right and wrong, good and bad, beautiful and ugly, and so on—are so inextricably bound up with your inner and outer life (for instance, with the structure of your motivations as well as with which actions you perform) that there is no practical way to just delete your values, without puting anything in their place, and still live a recognizably human life.

However, it may be possible to develop the practice of substituting for those value judgments you express in your speech and thought the factual judgments you would use to justify your value judgments. So, for instance, instead of saying (or thinking) that abortion is *morally wrong* (a value judgment), you could say that abortion generally results in the destruction of a fetus which hasn't yet intentionally done anything to cause pain and which has the potential to become a normal, conscious adult human being (a factual judgment), and that women are traumatized by allowing their fetuses to be killed (a factual judgment). Or, instead of saying that abortion is *morally permissible* (a value judgment), you could say that a fetus is not a conscious being (a factual judgment) and that, generally, women are more traumatized by giving birth to unwanted children than by aborting unwanted fetuses (a factual judgment). (Note that calling a judgment *factual* does not by itself imply that the judgment is correct but, merely, that it is a judgment about *facts*. Thus some factual judgments are true, some false, depending on what the *actual* facts are.)

Similarly, instead of saying (or thinking) that it is *good* to be sincere in talking with other people (a value judgment), you could say that being sincere usually promotes mutual understanding and trust (a factual judgment). Instead of saying (or thinking) that Siesta Key is a *more beautiful* beach in Florida than Fort Lauderdale (a value judgment), you could say that Siesta Key is a wider beach and has whiter, cleaner sand (a factual judgment).

The crucial distinction for this exercise in substitution is that between values and facts. While it may be a difficult distinction, its basic contours can best be illustrated in terms of simple examples. The value judgment, for instance, that Siesta Key is *more beautiful* than Fort Lauderdale is a value judgment in that it expresses a pro (or con) attitude and in that there is no reason to think that the relationship, "more beautiful than," exists independently of such attitudes. The factual judgment that Siesta Key is a *wider* beach than Fort Lauderdale, on the other hand, is factual in that it describes a certain relationship that exists in the world without expressing a pro or con attitude toward that relationship.

It is essential to the meaning of a value judgment—but not to the meaning of a factual judgment—that it expresses a pro or con attitude. In the preceding examples, a con or pro attitude toward abortion, a pro attitude toward sincerity, and a pro attitude toward Siesta Key beach as compared to Fort Lauderdale beach.

In addition, there are accepted techniques for determining whether most factual judgments are true. To determine whether Siesta Key is a wider beach than Fort Lauderdale, we can measure them. Sometimes there are also accepted techniques for determining whether value judgments are true. Thus, we have accepted techniques for determining whether a strawberry is red and sweet, and a red, sweet strawberry will almost invariably taste *better* than a green, bitter one. However, whereas determining the truth of factual judgments

involves showing that other *factual* judgments are true, determining the truth of value judgments, if we can determine their
truth at all, rarely, if ever, involves showing that just other
value judgments are true. Rather, as in the strawberry example,
it involves showing that other *factual* judgments are true. It
seems, then, that factual judgments are more fundamental than
value judgments in that value judgments depend on factual
judgments, but not vice versa.

It is often more convenient to use a value judgment than to
report the factual evidence that we would give to justify it.
But, convenience aside, it is nearly always possible for us to
replace a value judgment with our factual evidence for it. In
other words, even though value judgments and factual judgments may *mean* different things, if the only *reasons* we would
give to support a value judgment are factual judgments, then
most of the time we could just report our factual evidence and
thereby avoid the value judgment.

There are two possible problems with this strategy of
substituting factual judgments for value judgments. First, the
demarcation between values and facts is often fuzzy. The judgment that dinner was delicious, for instance, is not easily clas-
sified as either evaluative or factual. Second, if we continue
the analysis of our techniques for determining the truth of
factual judgments far enough, perhaps all the way to the end
(if there is an end), value judgments may reemerge. For instance, our views about whether God exists (a factual matter)
may, in the final analysis, be influenced by our commitment to
the rule that, all else being equal, simpler explanations are
more worthy of belief than complex ones. And our commitment
to this (or some such) rule, may, again in the final analysis, be
an expression of our values.

Such complications suggest that it is difficult to draw a
sharp distinction between values and facts. However, they do
not show that the option of dropping the values we express in
our thoughts and judgments—at least temporarily, for the purpose of examining them—is unrealistic. Although the demarcation between values and facts may be fuzzy, and we may not
be able to define the difference precisely, we can distinguish
clear cases of values from clear cases of facts—an ability to

distinguish that must be more basic than the ability to define the distinction between value and fact, since to define this distinction we would first have to recognize clear cases of both values and facts, or else we wouldn't be able to understand the distinction our definition was designed to capture.

The ability to distinguish clear cases of values from clear cases of facts is all you need, theoretically, to replace your value judgments with factual judgments. Even if many cases are borderline, and even if some procedural values still lurk far in the background, you could step out of almost all of your inherited frameworks of values if you could drop all clear cases of value judgments and replace them with the underlying factual judgments you would ordinarily give to justify them. That is, if you could stop not only expressing your values to others but also thinking them privately to yourself, you could then examine and critically assess your previous involvement with your values, not through the tinted lenses that these values themselves provide, but from a vantage point beyond their scope.

Would the strategy of replacing value judgments with the underlying factual evidence on which they are based work across the board, or are there some cases where you couldn't make the replacement because you have no underlying reasons for your value judgments? For instance, suppose you think some painting is beautiful—not because of its colors, shapes, textures, and the relationships among its visual elements— that is, not because of anything about the way the painting looks—but "just because." Your evaluation of the painting, in this case, is arbitrary in that it is independent of the painting's properties as well as independent of any further value considerations. If the only reason for saying that evaluations are not expendable is that we need them to make arbitrary evaluative judgments, then the question is whether we can get along as well or better without making arbitrary evaluative judgments. It seems we can.

A second possibility is that you have factual evidence for your value judgment that the painting is beautiful (so your judgment is not arbitrary), but you can't say what your evidence is and so you can't substitute your factual evidence for your value judgment. In this case, since your value judgment is not arbitrary, you would lose something if you jettisoned it without replacing it. And since you can't say what the factual evidence is upon which your value judgments are based (even though we are now supposing there is such evidence), you can't replace your judgment with a report of this evidence.

But, in that case, your inability to report the factual evidence underlying your value judgment must be either because you don't know what that evidence is or because you know what it is but can't put it into words. If you don't know what the facts underlying your value judgment are, how then do you know that there are any facts underlying your value judgment? If your assumption that your evaluation is grounded in facts is itself (so far as you know) arbitrary, then so is your value judgment. If, on the other hand, you have factual evidence *that you have factual evidence*, then you can report that *secondary* factual evidence instead of the value judgment.

Suppose, for instance, that you have factual evidence, you know that you have such evidence (perhaps by knowing what it is), but you can't put your evidence into words. Then you could at least put *that* into words. Instead of saying that you like the painting because it is beautiful, you could say that you like it for reasons you can't put into words. It's not clear that the first way of expressing yourself—evaluatively—is any better than the second way of expressing yourself—factually. Hence, it's hard to see what you would lose by dropping the evaluation.

A final possibility is that you have evidence for your value judgment (so it is not arbitrary), but your evidence is not factual evidence. What, then, could your evidence be? The only thing it seems it could be is simply your perception that the painting is beautiful, not because of any of its factual properties, but just beautiful per se.

The question, then, would be how you get access to this mysterious "evidence" that is not factual evidence. Our ordinary sense organs are capable of responding just to factual stimulation—sound waves, light waves, pressure, and so on. If you have access to evidence that is not ultimately physical stimulation, then it must be because you have a special organ for acquiring such evidence. Some people have actually thought that we do have "evaluative organs" (and some, perhaps, still think this); for instance, some ethicists used to think that, in addition to the senses we share with the higher animals, humans have a "moral sense." But no one has ever been able to locate this phantom organ or explain how it works to pick up evaluative information from the world. Today, few people are persuaded by such theories.

If you always give the factual reasons for your value judgments instead of making the value judgments themselves, *you* will stick to the facts. Other people, if they wanted to, could draw their own evaluative conclusions. However, the people to whom you would communicate factually would not *have to* draw their own evaluative conclusions. They could, if they wanted to, stick to the facts and respond accordingly. For instance, if instead of telling people that you are good at chess, you told them that you are a grand master, then they, instead of concluding that you are good at chess, could turn down your offer to play for money. Their reason would not have to be (the evaluative one) that you are better than they are, but rather (the factual one) that if they play against you, they would probably lose. Thus, the policy of substituting factual judgments for value judgments is not necessarily just a way of shuffling value judgments around—moving them, say, from your mouth to other mouths—but potentially of eliminating altogether those value judgments we express to one another.

Even so, you might well have grave doubts about whether this program of substituting factual judgments for value judgments is realistic. Perhaps, with practice, you could stop expressing your values to others. But could you also stop thinking value judgments privately to yourself? And even if you could, wouldn't the practice of doing so impoverish your life?

The question now is not just one of communication. You could stop making value judgments to others simply by being quiet. To stop making them to yourself, you would have to stop *thinking* them—you would have to drop all your evaluative beliefs. If the earlier policy of not communicating your values to others would be a significant step, this new policy of not even thinking them would be a monumental leap.

Making a value judgment to yourself is a lot like "communicating to yourself." (As someone once remarked, "How do I know what I'm thinking until I hear what I'm saying?") To communicate with others you have to form the judgment and also express it publicly, whereas to communicate with yourself you have only to form the judgment—to think it. Still, if you could live your life without communicating your values to others, couldn't you live your life—perhaps as easily—without communicating them to yourself?

Surprisingly, you could live your life almost as easily and in exactly the same way. However difficult it might be in practice to break the habit of making value judgments, in theory you could refrain from making them. Either you could be (internally) "silent" or you could think only about the relevant underlying facts. It would be difficult, since our evaluative habits are so deeply ingrained and since speech is more easily controlled than thought. But since external silence or the substitution of factual judgments for overt value judgments is possible, internal silence or a similar internal substitution must also be possible, and for exactly the same reasons. Thus, you could eliminate all clear cases of value judgments—without qualification (except perhaps for the procedural value judgments mentioned earlier that may underlie our methods for determining facts).

It is sometimes said that a life without values would be impossible, or, at least, not recognizably human. Interestingly, though, if you could refrain from making (even thinking) any value judgments, others could as well. In theory, then, we could see ourselves and the world without values—seemingly without losing anything that is essential to our lives.

The elimination of all value judgments (including those that are merely thought) is tantamount to the elimination of values. For where do values exist except in our minds? Thus, we could, in theory, take the truly radical step of actually creating a recognizably human world without any values whatsoever—not just a world without objective values (we may already have that) but a world without even subjective values.

In a world without values we would have to stop judging ourselves and each other evaluatively. When you judge yourself evaluately, you compare yourself either to yourself at a different time, or to someone else, or to some idealized person—perhaps the "you" that you, your family, or your friends would like you to be. Since most of us spend a lot of time and energy in the often unpleasant task of comparing ourselves evaluatively, our lives would be quite different if we stopped. Since no one likes to be constantly judged, and self-judgment can be more oppressive than external evaluation, it seems that to this extent at least, our lives might be less oppressive and happier if we gave up comparing ourselves evaluatively.

Even were we to give up judging ourselves evaluatively, we could still make factual comparisons, even ones right on the threshhold of being evaluative. For instance, the judgment that you got an A in every course you took last semester (whether or not it is true) is a factual judgment. So is the judgment that someone else thinks you are a good student. For that matter, so is the judgment that you once thought you were a good student, if you are simply reporting what you once thought and not endorsing the thought. On the other hand, the (endorsed) judgment that you actually are a good student is evaluative.

In sum, if you gave up comparing yourself and others evaluatively, you could still make factual comparisons. The only difference (perhaps an important one) is that you would not express any pro or con attitude on the value of these comparisons. For instance, you could note that your cumulative grade average in college is B+, as compared to the collegewide average of C+, but you could not even *think* that it is *better* to have a higher than a lower grade average. You could, of course, recognize that graduates with higher averages tend to get higher paying jobs, but you could not even think that it is good to get a higher paying job.

It may seem, then, that dropping all evaluative comparisons would radically undercut your motivation. If you didn't think that getting a B+ is better than getting a B–, what possible motive could you have to do the extra work to get a

B+? Surprisingly, your motives would probably remain about the same. For instance, you might do the extra work because you want a higher salaried job after you graduate. But why want a higher salaried job if it isn't *better* than a lower salaried job? Again, for your same old reasons: say, because then you will have enough money to buy new clothes and pay the rent for the house you prefer to live in. But why want those things if they are not *better*? Ultimately: because you think they will please you.

Isn't it *better* to be pleased than not? Perhaps. But the mere fact that something pleases you (a factual matter) may be motive enough for doing it. The value judgment that it is better to do things that please you is motivationally redundant. There is, then, no reason to think that dropping all value judgments would undercut your motivation to pursue your goals. You would be deprived of evaluative reasons for being motivated, but to the extent that you rely on such reasons, they could easily be replaced by factual reasons. In sum, so far as motivation is concerned, nothing would be lost.

Would anything be added by seeing yourself without values? Two things: clarity and immediacy. Dropping evaluative judgments and replacing them with the factual judgments on which they are based would force you to get clearer about why you have the preferences and aversions you do. The evaluative judgment, "Because it's good (or bad)," as a response to the question of why you like (or dislike) something is about as informative as saying, "Just because." The factual basis for your evaluation will almost always be more informative.

With evaluations available, often we don't go to the trouble of getting clear about what lies behind them. We're lazy and it's easier to give our evaluative summation and leave the factual underpinnings implicit and murky. This makes evaluation dangerous as a self-deceptive tool. For instance, someone who is suffering from extreme guilt can say "I'm bad," rather than focusing on the underlying cause of the guilt, such as parental disapproval. Or, a student doing poorly in a class can say, "I'm a bad student," rather than focusing on the facts underlying the problem, such as ineffective study habits. Negative evaluations thus often get locked into our psyches and block access to the neutral factual information that provoked them in the first place. That's why in psychotherapy, for instance, a person who thinks he is "bad" can contribute importantly to his cure by simply telling the therapist (and himself) exactly (and neutrally) what lies behind his self-condemnation.

Factual judgments are more immediate than value judgments because they are more fundamental. The evaluative judgment that something is *good* is often little more than an objectified version of the more personal judgment that you liked it. The more immediate fact is that you liked it. The judgment that it is good is evaluative packaging. Just as people in positions of authority often wear uniforms to impress us, it is as if we dress up our naked personal preferences in objective trappings before sending them out into the world.

The depersonalized and objectifying features of value judgments are a distancing mechanism—a way of going beyond and away from our personal reactions. In distancing ourselves from our personal preferences through evaluative language, we camouflage the fact that we are claiming more than mere personal preference would warrant. The evaluative move is thus a way not only of adding an additional theoretical layer to the ways we conceptualize the psychological reality of our lives, but also a covert way of portraying our personal preferences as if they were something more and grander than they are.

Unclothed from your values, you would stand naked, no longer judging your life evaluatively, but simply living it; no longer judging the lives of others evaluatively, but simply interacting with them (or not). It seems, then, that replacing your value judgments with the factual evidence that supports them is not only theoretically possible, but a way of stepping outside your value frameworks and seeing yourself and your values more neutrally.

There is a second way of getting outside the framework of your values. This way does not require that you stop making value judgments but only that you (nonevaluatively) watch yourself making them. That is, you try to understand the role of your values in your life, not by taking anything away from your thought or behavior (such as your value judgments) but by adding something to them: a nonjudging awareness of exactly what you are doing and why you are doing it, so that you can understand experientially what your values are and how they affect your life and the lives of others.

Most of us can separate—dissociate—a part of our subjective lives from the rest of ourselves. The part you would dissociate, then, becomes a neutral watcher of the rest of your experience and behavior, including your judging behavior. That is, with the part of your awareness that is dissociated from the rest, you look at everything in which you are involved without saying yes or no to anything that happens, to what you do, to what happens to you, to your experiences, to what other people do, and so on. Your pleasures, pains, sensations, thoughts, and emotions are allowed to continue without this dissociated part of yourself—the "watcher"—trying to direct the show. The watcher is simply there, with your life, aware of what is happening, but not judging it, perhaps more aware of yourself than you ordinarily are, even than you've ever been, because now your values are out of the way. Yet the watcher is just a neutral observer, not trying to make anything happen, not trying to stop anything from happening, just watching. Even when this neutral part of you is aware that another part of you is involved in evaluative judgments, the neutral part does not need to participate in those judgments— rather, it can just watch the judging without either identifying with it or judging it. For instance, if this neutral part of you is aware that another part of you is proud (a judgmental reaction), it does not have to identify with the pride or judge it— it can just watch.

The question, then, is whether you can locate within yourself a neutral center of awareness that is beyond all your theories and answers about good and bad, right and wrong, beautiful and ugly, and so on. And can you be neutral with yourself for long enough that your values and judgments seem like the values and judgments of someone else—items in the world that arouse your interest, that you are aware of and aware of how they affect the bodies and minds you are watching? In other words, can you dissociate a part of yourself that is just a presence, aware of everything going on at the moment, but not identified with anything, beyond values and theories and attitudes and answers? Can you be consumed by the utterly simple, unuttered question, "What is this?" Next moment: "And what is this?" "And this?" "And this?"—never gathering it all up, never theorizing, just watching every experience, emotion, thought, and movement? In short, can you watch your values without identifying with them, without the neutral watcher within you owning them as *its* values?

This may seem a strange and artificial exercise, but it can be revealing. If the values you are watching are not really "your" values—not the values of the watcher, anyway— inevitably the question arises: If I am the watcher, who, then, is the other? Who is the one being watched, the conditioned one, the posturing one, the one with the answers, the views, with the yes's and no's, this strange alien person that from this neutral perspective hardly even seems a person, but, rather, more like an organism, a biological and psychological mechanism, programmed by its culture like some kind of elaborate wind-up toy, different now from you-the-watcher? If without thinking or theorizing, without gathering up the insights, you can just watch each moment come and go, letting that awareness in you be distanced from what is being watched, freed of that body-mind complex, then later when you return to the values that before were so familiar, so close to you they stuck like glue, they are now all strangeness.

What is your life from this neutral vantage point that is not even really a vantage point on a life that is not even "your" life? What can you learn? Perhaps that "you," the watcher, do not feel like the same person as this mind-body complex you are watching, that what you are watching is not only a conditioned machine, but an unskillful, clumsy machine (not that you judge this, but, rather, you just see the machine trying for a certain effect as if it—the machine—originated the trying and then you see it failing by doing something that will never bring about the desired effect but exactly the opposite). Perhaps, as you watch, you can see all the genuine- ness in the situation you are watching leak away, never expressed, never even noticed by the bungling machine lumbering through a life, hurting, often without even noticing that it is hurting. Perhaps you see that what you are watching doesn't mesh well with its environment because it is not just happening, but awkwardly trying for various effects that it unskillfully acts (reacts) to try to bring about, rarely seeing situations clearly for what they are because this thing sees everything only through a cloudy glass of conditioned needs.

If you can observe yourself in this way for a few minutes, even for one minute, even for seven seconds, then for at least that length of time, you are out of the framework of values within which the thing you are watching—what you used to call "yourself"—lives its life. For a time, you—the neutral watcher—are out of it, free from it, but not forever, not even for long, because it sucks you up again as soon as your awareness wavers, like some giant vacuum cleaner that gathers dirt but is unable to clean itself, a valuer, engaged in the world but out of sync, a wobble, every action a reaction, nothing original, nothing new, an echo, distorted, unskillful, full of pain, causing pain, bungling, forever bungling . . . on the way to the saw.

FURTHER READING

Daniel Kolak and Raymond Martin's *The Experience of Philosophy*, Wadsworth, 1990, is a companion reader to the present book. Its sections, which correspond to the chapters of this book, include 64 selections by philosophers (including Plato, Thomas Aquinas, René Descartes, Blaise Pascal, John Locke, George Berkeley, David Hume, Immanuel Kant, John Stuart Mill, Friedrich Neitzsche, William James, Bertrand Russell, Jean-Paul Sartre, Robert Nozick, Thomas Nagel, Raymond Smullyan, Richard Taylor, John Hick, John Perry, Daniel C. Dennett, Paul Churchland, Jonathan Bennett, Gilbert Harman, D. M. Armstrong, Alvin Plantinga, Jonathan Glover, Paul Teller, Frank Jackson, Arnold Zuboff, and Douglas Hofstadter), scientists (including Stanley Milgram, Paul Davies, Richard Dawkins, and Freeman Dyson), and writers (including Leo Tolstoy, Mark Twain, H. L. Mencken, Albert Camus, Milan Kundera, and Adrienne Rich).

Introduction

Bertrand Russell, one of this century's most brilliant philosophers, won a Nobel Prize for literature. He wrote two books that provide excellent access to philosophy: *Problems of Philosophy* (Oxford, 1959), which takes a direct, "problems approach," and *History of Western Philosophy* (Simon & Schuster, 1945), which takes a historical approach. The "problems" book is brief; the history book can serve as a superb text on the history of Western thought. Both are written with grace, insight, and humor.

Thomas Nagel's *What Does It All Mean?* (Oxford, 1986) is

an accessible, interesting, and very short introduction to philosophy. Those who like puzzles and paradoxes will find a good selection in the final section of *Introduction to Philosophy*, edited by John Perry and Michael Bratman (Oxford, 1986). One of the best compact overviews of the different areas of philosophy, which includes sections on philosophical terminology and both formal and informal logic, is Samuel Gorovitz et al., *Philosophical Analysis*, 3d ed. (Random House, 1979). Michael Scriven's amusing *Reasoning* (McGraw-Hill, 1976) and Evelyn Barker's *Everyday Reasoning* (Prentice-Hall, 1981) are more extensive primers on informal logic. An offbeat and humorous approach to introductory logic is *Logic For An Overcast Tuesday* by Robert J. Rafalko (Wadsworth, 1990).

Those who would like to be introduced to philosophy by Socrates himself can find the gadfly alive and still stinging in Plato's dialogs. The best place to start is the *Euthyphro* where, among other things, Socrates detaches ethics from theology with one penetrating question. Socrates did not answer his question, and Socrates is, of course, dead; but more than 2000 years later his question still lives. The moving story of Socrates' trial, imprisonment, and death is told in the *Apology*, *Crito*, and *Phaedo*.

Where

In the forty pages of *Cosmic View: The Universe in Forty Jumps* (Day, 1957), Kees Boeke puts the immense scale of the universe into perspective all the way from the galaxies to the center of an atom. In *Powers of Ten* (Freeman, 1982) Philip Morrison takes you on a pictorial tour of the cosmos that starts with two picnickers on a blanket in a park in Chicago, moves all the way up to the swirling galaxies and beyond, and then back down to the interior of one of the picnicker's hands, all the way into the heart of an atom.

E. A. Abbott's 19th-century classic *Flatland* (Dover, 1952) is probably the most delightful book ever written on space and dimensionality. Abbott's story is a touching fantasy about a square who lives in a two-dimensional world until the day he is whisked into the third dimension. When he returns to Flatland, he has trouble convincing his friends to admit even the possibility that space could have three dimensions.

Another superb fantasy is George Gamow's *Mr. Tompkins in Wonderland* (Cambridge, 1940). Written in the style of a third-grade primer, it illustrates without any technical language some of the most startling implications of living in an Einsteinian universe.

Those who want a more sophisticated treatment should read Hans Reichenbach's *Philosophy of Space and Time* (Dover, 1958), a modern classic that takes the reader on a mind-bending odyssey through the topology of space and time. For readers interested in visualizing the topological twist of the "uncrossable river" story, the best is *A Topological Picturebook* by George K. Francis (Springer-Verlag, 1987), a delightful, hands-on, how-to book on drawing mathematical pictures, with lots of mind-bending pictures.

For an easy and thoroughly exciting account of the concept of infinity, nothing beats Constance Reid's *Introduction to Higher Mathematics for the General Reader* (Thomas Y. Crowell, 1959) except, perhaps, Tobias Danzig's rather more sophisticated but still comprehensible treatise *Number*, 4th ed. (Macmillan, 1967), which Einstein himself called the greatest book about mathematics he ever read.

For a sweeping historical panorama of different models of the cosmos, see Milton Munitz, *Theories of the Universe* (Free Press, 1957).

Daniel C. Dennett's "Where Am I?" originally published in *Brainstorms* (Bradford Books, 1978) and reprinted in Kolak and Martin, eds., *The Experience of Philosophy* (Wadsworth, 1990) brings to light the unobvious mystery of how we locate ourselves. By imagining a situation in which his body is separated from his brain, Dennett shows why even the most obvious apparent fact about you, expressed by your avowal, "I am here," is deeply questionable.

When

Albert Einstein's *Relativity* (Crown, 1961) is a popular exposition of relativity by its originator. In *The Direction of*

Time (University of California, 1971), Hans Reichenbach offers a historical survey of the concept of time leading up to the advent of quantum mechanics.

For those who want an elementary account, Bertrand Russell's *The ABC of Relativity* (Signet, 1959) is one of the simplest and most readable versions of Einstein's theory. *Relativity in Illustrations* (New York University Press, 1962), by Jacob Schwartz, illustrates, using completely nontechnical language and lots of pictures and diagrams, the most basic parts of relativity.

In "Time," originally published in *God and the New Physics* (Simon & Schuster, 1983) and reprinted in Kolak and Martin, eds., *The Experience of Philosophy*, the theoretical physicist and brilliant expositor of contemporary physics, Paul Davies, describes the startling discoveries recent physics has made about the nature of time. Steven Hawking's *A Brief History of Time* (Bantam Books, 1988) is a scientifically provocative but historically somewhat inaccurate account by one of the best living physicists.

For an intriguing exploration of the relationship among time, thought, and consciousness, see *The Ending of Time* (Harper & Row, 1985), by experiential philosopher J. Krishnamurti and theoretical physicist David Bohm.

Who

The modern discussion of personal identity began with John Locke's "Of Identity and Diversity," Chapter 27 of Book II of *Essay Concerning Human Understanding* (Awnsham & Churchil, 2nd ed., 1694; Oxford, 1979). For this and a good selection of the historically important literature until 1971, see John Perry's *Personal Identity* (University of California Press, 1975). Perry's own *A Dialogue on Personal Identity and Immortality* (Hackett, 1978) is an accessible, brief dramatization of the major contemporary concerns. For an actual exchange between two contemporary philosophers, see Richard Swinburne and Sydney Shoemaker, *Personal Identity* (Blackwell, 1984), in which each philosopher writes his views and then comments critically on the other's essay.

Douglas Hofstadter and Daniel Dennett put together what is probably the most dazzling and mind-jolting philosophy anthology ever collected for those beginning to question the nature of self and consciousness, *The Mind's I* (Basic Books, 1981). It is a fascinating mix of philosophy, computer science, biology, psychology, and literature. A more technical but still excellent anthology that focuses specifically on the question of personal identity is Amélie Rorty, ed., *The Identities of Persons* (University of California Press, 1976).

Daniel Kolak and Raymond Martin, eds., *Self and Identity: Contemporary Philosophical Issues* (Macmillan, 1990) is a comprehensive anthology of current philosophical thought on the problems of unity of consciousness, personal identity, and self.

On the interesting idea that you don't even have a self, see David Hume's classic statement in Part IV, Book I, and the Appendix of *A Treatise of Human Nature*, first published in 1739 and 1740 (2nd ed., Oxford, 1978) and Peter Unger's recent and even more dramatic "I Do Not Exist," in G. F. MacDonald, ed., *Perception and Identity* (Cornell University Press, 1979, pp. 235–251), which takes the idea one provocative step further.

Daniel C. Dennett, in "The Origins of Selves," *Cogito*, 1990, reprinted in Kolak and Martin, eds., *Self and Identity* (Macmillan, 1990), argues that just as novelists invent fictional characters, so the human brain invents the fiction of self.

Thomas Nagel's "Brain Bisection and the Unity of Consciousness" in *Mortal Questions* (Cambridge University Press, 1979) is an intriguing foray into the problems about identity raised by *literally mind-splitting* neurosurgery.

Chapter 1 of Robert Nozick's remarkably expansive and synthetic *Philosophical Explanations* (Harvard University Press, 1981) starts with the basics of personal identity and quickly accelerates to making state-of-the-art original contributions. An innovative and widely discussed work is the personal identity section (Chapters 10–13) of Derek Parfit's *Reasons and Persons* (Oxford, 1984). Peter Unger's "Consciousness and Self Identity" (*Midwest Studies in Philosophy* 10 [1986]: 63–100) explores the interesting question of why we respond to puzzles about personal identity in the ways we do.

Unger's recent *Identity, Consciousness and Value* (Oxford, 1990), in a dramatic departure from his earlier radical views, includes the best defense ever of the physical view of personal identity.

In "Personal Identity and Causality: Becoming Unglued" (*American Philosophical Quarterly* 24 [1987]: 337–347), the authors of the present book argue that there is much less that is essential to our identities over time than either laypersons or philosophers ordinarily assume. Raymond Martin has explored the question of what matters in our continuing survival as persons over time in "Memory, Connecting, and What Matters in Survival" (*Australasian Journal of Philosophy* 65 [1987]: 82–97), "Identity and Survival: The Persons We Most Want to Be," in Kolak and Martin, eds., *The Experience of Philosophy* (Wadsworth, 1990), and "Identity, Transformation, and What Matters in Survival," in Kolak and Martin, eds., *Self and Identity* (Macmillan, 1990), and "Identity's Crisis" (*Philosophical Studies* 53 [1988]: 295–307). Daniel Kolak's forthcoming novel *The Train*, a philosophical journey into the question of personal identity, is about a man who misses enlightenment by a beltloop.

In Milan Kundera's "The Hitchhiking Game," in *Laughable Loves* (Knopf, 1974) and reprinted in Kolak and Martin, eds., *The Experience of Philosophy* (Wadsworth, 1990), a couple innocently begin playing a game about their identities which gets deeper and deeper, revealing masks beneath masks, until finally they are no longer sure of what the truth is or of who they really are.

Two recent contributions that combine perspectives from differing philosophical traditions—the analytic and the phenomenological—are Charles Taylor's *Sources of the Self* (Harvard, 1989) and Richard Rorty's *Contingency, Irony and Solidarity* (Cambridge University Press, 1989). Joseph Margolis's *Science Without Unity* (Basil Blackwell, 1987) also contains a large section devoted to problems of self.

For a lucid and insightful exploration of the mysterious connection between self and quantum mechanics, see Allen Stairs, "Quantum Mechanics, Mind, and Self," in Kolak and Martin, eds., *Self and Identity* (Macmillan, 1990).

Knowledge

The first two sections of René Descartes's *Meditations on First Philosophy* (Cambridge University Press, 1986), first published in 1640, changed the face of modern philosophy by bringing questions about both the nature and extent of human knowledge to the center of philosophical discussion. Without any technical jargon, these dozen or so pages can still pull the rug, and even the floor, right out from under anyone who reads them. Two readable and interesting commentaries on Descartes are Fred Feldman's *A Cartesian Introduction to Philosophy* (McGraw-Hill, 1986) and Harry Frankfurt's *Demons, Dreamers and Madmen* (Bobbs-Merrill, 1970).

A good introduction to the study of knowledge is W. V. Quine and J. S. Ullian, *The Web of Belief*, 2nd ed. (Random House, 1978). Much of the important 20th-century work on perception, up to 1964, is well represented in R. J. Swartz, ed., *Perceiving, Sensing and Knowing* (Anchor, 1965). Two more recent anthologies are Roderick Chisholm and Robert Swartz, eds., *Empirical Knowledge: Readings from Contemporary Sources* (Prentice-Hall, 1973) and George Pappas and Marshall Swain, eds., *Essays on Knowledge and Justification* (Cornell University Press, 1978). Significant recent developments may be found in Fred Dretske's readable *Seeing and Knowing* (University of Chicago Press, 1969), Dretske's *Knowledge and the Flow of Information* (M.I.T., 1981), Robert Nozick's *Philosophical Explanations* (Harvard University Press, 1981), Keith Lehrer's *Knowledge* (Oxford, 1974), and Peter Unger's *Ignorance* (Oxford, 1975).

Two useful introductions to the logic of scientific reasoning are Brian Skyrms's *Choice and Chance*, 2d ed. (Dickinson, 1975) and Ronald Giere's *Understanding Scientific Reasoning*, 2d ed. (Holt, Rinehart & Winston, 1984).

W. V. O. Quine's *From a Logical Point of View* (Harvard University Press, 1953) and his *Ontological Relativity and Other Essays* (Columbia University Press, 1969) provide an excellent example of a hard-nosed scientific approach by one of the most influential of today's philosophers, whereas Thomas Kuhn's *The Structure of Scientific Revolutions*, 2d ed. (University of

Chicago Press, 1970) delivers a mighty blow to the idea that science is objective. Kuhn's book has become one of the most widely discussed philosophy books of the last several decades. Israel Scheffler responds lucidly to Kuhn's arguments in his *Science and Subjectivity,* 2d ed. (Hackett, 1982). Paul Feyerabend mounts the attack against scientific objectivity anew in *Against Method* (Humanities Press, 1975) and in many other stimulating and often beautifully outrageous books and papers.

The problem of knowing things historically and the traditional approaches to solving it are nicely summarized in William Dray's *Philosophy of History* (Prentice-Hall, 1964) and William Dray, ed., *Philosophical Analysis and History* (Harper & Row, 1966), whereas Raymond Martin argues for a new approach to the philosophy of history in *The Past Within Us* (Princeton University Press, 1989).

God

One of the most provocative and irreverent attacks ever on belief in God is Bertrand Russell's "Why I Am Not a Christian" in *Why I Am Not a Christian and Other Essays on Religion and Related Topics* (Allen & Unwin, 1957). Ernest Nagel's "A Defense of Atheism," originally in J. E. Fairchild, ed., *Basic Beliefs* (Sheridan House, 1959) and frequently reprinted, is a classic defense of the nonbeliever's position. More lengthy but equally powerful treatments can be found in Michael Scriven's *Primary Philosophy* (McGraw-Hill, 1975), Wallace E. Matson's *The Existence of God* (Cornell University Press, 1965), and J. L. Mackie's *The Miracle of Theism* (Oxford, 1982). J. C. A. Gaskin's *The Varieties of Unbelief* (Macmillan, 1989) is an historically comprehensive anthology of religious skepticism from Epicurus to Sartre.

For a philosophically sophisticated defense of religious belief, one can do no better than Alvin Plantiga's *God, Freedom and Evil* (Eerdmans, 1977) and his *Faith and Rationality* (Notre Dame, 1983), Richard Swinburne's *Coherence of Theism* (Oxford, 1977) and his *Faith and Reason* (Oxford, 1981), and William Alston's *Religious Belief and Philosophical Thought*

(Harcourt Brace Jovanovich, 1963).

Three classic western philosophical accounts sympathetic to faith, religious experience, and mysticism are Søren Kierkegaard's 19th-century classic *Concluding Unscientific Postscript* (Princeton University Press, 1969); William James's *The Varieties of Religious Experience* (Longmans, Green, 1902); and W. T. Stace's provocative *Mysticism and Philosophy* (Lippincott, 1960). Abbott's *Flatland*, mentioned above, is also highly relevant as allegory. For an innovative and balanced account of the mystic's claim to have experienced ultimate reality, see Robert Nozick's treatment in *Philosophical Explanations* (Harvard University Press, 1981). An excellent comprehensive anthology is Terence Penelhum, ed., *Faith* (Macmillan, 1989).

The classic discussion of the argument for God based on apparent design in the universe is David Hume's *Dialogues Concerning Natural Religion*, originally published in 1776 and available in many suitable editions. Richard Taylor, in *Metaphysics*, 3d ed. (Prentice-Hall, 1983), gives an interesting recent defense of the argument for God based on apparent design in the universe. To see how a top-flight physicist makes room for God in the modern scientific world, see Freeman Dyson's beautifully written *Infinite in All Directions* (Harper & Row, 1988).

A different sort of attack on religious belief, together with insightful discussions of the possibilities for living without it, can be found in any one of J. Krishnamurti's books, such as his delightfully accessible *Think on These Things* (Harper & Row, 1964) and his *Freedom from the Known* (Harper & Row, 1969). Nelson Pike's *God and Evil* (Prentice-Hall, 1964), with its helpful bibliography, is an excellent place to begin a more careful study of the problem of evil and the various replies to it.

An excellent place to begin thinking about the question of free will is Clarence Darrow's summation to the jury in the famous Leopold and Loeb case, one of the most gripping philosophical speeches of all time, published in Arthur Weinberg, ed., *Attorney for the Damned* (Simon & Schuster, 1957). Several excellent older anthologies on free will include Bernard Berofsky, ed., *Free Will and Determinism* (Harper & Row,

1966); Sidney Hook, ed., *Determinism and Freedom in the Age of Modern Science* (New York University Press, 1958); Keith Lehrer, ed., *Freedom and Determinism* (Random House, 1966); Sidney Morgenbesser and James Walsh, eds., *Free Will* (Prentice-Hall, 1962); and D. F. Pears, *Freedom and the Will* (St. Martin's Press, 1963). The best recent anthology is Gary Watson, ed., *Free Will* (Oxford, 1982). Peter van Inwagen's *Essay on Free Will* (Oxford, 1983) is a sophisticated and somewhat technical but important study of free will. Daniel Dennett's *Elbow Room* (M.I.T., 1984) is an extremely readable defense of free will. An unusual and insightful exploration of the importance of free will may be found in Susan Wolf's "The Importance of Free Will" (*Mind* 90 [1981]: 378–386).

Finally, no student should even *think* about leaving a university and going out into the world without reading and pondering Stanley Milgram's *Obedience to Authority* (Harper & Row, 1975).

Reality

The best way to get access to Western thought on the nature of reality is to study the great philosophers, especially Plato's *Phaedo, Republic, Parmenides, Thaetetus,* and *Sophist;* Aristotle's *Categories, Posterior Analytics, Physics, De Anima,* and *Metaphysics;* René Descartes's *Meditations, Principles,* and *The World;* G. W. Leibnitz's *Monadology;* John Locke's *Essay Concerning Human Understanding;* George Berkeley's *The Principles of Human Knowledge* and his *Three Dialogues Between Hylas and Philonous;* David Hume's *Treatise of Human Nature* and *Inquiry Concerning Human Understanding;* and Immanuel Kant's *Critique of Pure Reason.*

Some extremely useful contemporary summaries of the major metaphysical issues include Richard Taylor's *Metaphysics,* 3d ed. (Prentice-Hall, 1983) and D. W. Hamlyn's *Metaphysics* (Cambridge University Press, 1984). Readable recent surveys include Bruce Aune, *Metaphysics: The Elements* (University of Minnesota Press, 1985) and W. R. Carter, *The Elements of Metaphysics* (McGraw-Hill, 1990).

Raymond Smullyan, in "Dream or Reality," from *5000 B.C.*

(St. Martins, 1983), Daniel Kolak, in "The Experiment," in *Sirius*, no. 38, 1979, and Robert Nozick, in "Fiction," in *Ploughshares*, Fall, 1980, all reprinted in Kolak and Martin, eds., *The Experience of Philosophy* (Wadsworth, 1990), explore one of the oldest themes in history—that reality is a dream.

The important 20th-century literature tends to be rather technical and would be difficult reading for nonphilosophers. But for those who wish to be up to date on the basic issues and who are willing to make the effort, the following are highly recommended: G. Frege's "Sense and Reference" in P. Geach and M. Black, eds., *Translations from the Philosophical Writings of Gottlob Frege*, 2d ed. (Blackwell, 1970); B. Russell, "On Denoting" (*Mind* 14 [1905]: 479–493); P. Strawson, "On Referring" (*Mind* 59 [1950]: 320–344); W. Quine, *From a Logical Point of View* (Harvard University Press, 1953), especially Chapters 1, 2, and 8; his "Translation and Meaning" in *Word and Object* (M.I.T., 1960); his "On the Reasons for the Indeterminacy of Translation" (*Journal of Philosophy* 67 [1967]: 178–183); and his "Ontological Relativity" in Quine, *Ontological Relativity and Other Essays* (Columbia University Press, 1969); H. Grice and P. Strawson, "In Defense of a Dogma" (*Philosophical Review* 65 [1956]: 141–158); H. Grice, "Meaning" (*Philosophical Review* 66 [1957]: 377–388); S. Kripke, *Naming and Necessity* (Harvard University Press, 1980) and his *Wittgenstein on Rules and Private Language* (Harvard University Press, 1982); B. Brody, *Identity and Essence* (Princeton University Press, 1980), especially Chapters 1–5; David Lewis, "New Work for a Theory of Universals" (*Australasian Journal of Philosophy* 61 [1983]: 343–377); D. Davidson, "Truth and Meaning" (*Synthese* 17 [1967]: 304–323), his "True to the Facts" (*Journal of Philosophy* 66 [1969]: 748–764), and his "Reality Without Reference" in M. Platts, ed., *Reference, Truth, and Reality* (Routledge & Kegan Paul, 1980); R. Rorty, "The World Well Lost" (*Journal of Philosophy* 69 [1972]: 649–665); M. Dummett's "Realism" in *Truth and Other Enigmas* (Harvard University Press, 1978); H. Putnam, *Meaning and the Moral Sciences* (Routledge & Kegan Paul, 1978), especially Parts I and IV; J. L. Mackie, *The Cement of the Universe* (Oxford, 1974), especially Chapters 2, 3, and 7; and Terrence Parsons,

Nonexistent Objects (Yale University Press, 1980). For excellent discussions of the nature of reality, see Milton Munitz's *Cosmic Understanding* (Princeton University Press, 1990) and *The Question of Reality* (Princeton University Press, 1990).

Experience

The relationship between consciousness and physiology has been much discussed by 20th-century philosophers. Three classic treatments are L. Wittgenstein's *Philosophical Investigations* (Blackwell, 1953), Gilbert Ryle's *Concept of Mind* (Hutchinson, 1949), and W. Sellers's "Empiricism and the Philosophy of Mind" in *Science, Perception, and Reality* (Routledge & Kegan Paul, 1971).

The main traditional issue was whether conscious states can be identified with brain states. Two excellent anthologies that represent the best thought on this issue are D. Rosenthal, ed., *Materialism and the Mind-Body Problem* (Prentice-Hall, 1971) and J. O'Connor, ed., *Modern Materialism: Readings on the Mind-Body Identity* (Harcourt, Brace & World, 1969). Daniel Dennett's "Current Issues in the Philosophy of Mind" (*American Philosophical Quarterly* 15 [1978]: 249–261), an excellent source for students, is a clear and accessible account of how and why this main traditional issue became transformed in more recent debates.

Dennett and Hofstadter's *The Mind's I* (Basic Books, 1981) and Paul Churchland's *Matter and Consciousness*, rev. ed. (M.I.T., 1988) are also excellent places to begin the study of the relation between mind and brain. Other important work includes Daniel Dennett, *Brainstorms* (Bradford, 1978); J. Fodor's *The Language of Thought* (Harvard University Press, 1979) and his *Representations* (M.I.T., 1981) as well as his *Modularity of Mind* (M.I.T., 1983); and N. Block, "Troubles with Functionalism" (*Minnesota Studies in the Philosophy of Science* 9 [1978]: 261–325). Thomas Nagel's by now classic, "What Is It Like to Be a Bat?" *Philosophical Review*, October 1974, reprinted in Kolak and Martin, eds., *The Experience of Philosophy* (Wadsworth, 1990), and Nagel's more recent *The View from Nowhere* (Oxford, 1986) are intriguing attempts to state the antireductionist view that there is more to consciousness than what can be captured in our current scientific theories.

Two excellent experiential accounts that deconstruct interpretation and thought from immediate experience are D. E. Harding, *On Having No Head* (Harper & Row, 1972), an excerpt of which appears in *The Experience of Philosophy*, and Jean-Paul Sartre's philosophical novel *Nausea* (New Directions, 1964). Both dramatize the power and catharsis of confronting one's experience of the world directly rather than through theory.

Understanding

Emile Meyerson's classic *Identity and Reality* (Dover, 1962), originally published in 1906, is a historical and sophisticated yet accessible account of scientific explanation that raises the interesting question of where reductionism might lead. The novelist and philosopher Arthur Koestler is probably the best known critic of reductionism. His *Janus: A Summing Up* (Vintage, 1979) is one of his best, and, along with J. R. Smithies, he published the anthology *Beyond Reductionism* (Beacon Press, 1983). For a criticism of Koestler's approach, see Stephen Toulmin's amusing essay on Koestler in *The Return to Cosmology* (University of California Press, 1982).

Three recent philosophical contributions to the reductionism debate are Frank Jackson, "Epiphenomenal Qualia," *Philosophical Quarterly*, v. 32, 1982, Paul Churchland, "Reduction, Qualia, and the Direct Introspection of Brain States," *Journal of Philosophy*, v. 82, 1985, and Paul Teller, "Subjectivity," all included in Kolak and Martin, eds., *The Experience of Philosophy* (Wadsworth, 1990).

On the relationship between mind and nature, John Gribbin's *In Search of Schrödinger's Cat* (Bantam, 1984) is great fun. On this topic the works of Werner Heisenberg, Erwin Schrödinger, John Archibald Wheeler, and Paul Davies (listed under the next chapter) are all appropriate.

Nothingness

A good introduction to the view that consciousness is necessary for the universe to exist is G. Gale, "The Anthropic Principle" (*Scientific American* 254 [Dec. 1981]: 154–171). The most comprehensive book on the Anthropic Principle is J. Barrow and F. Tippler's *Anthropic Cosmological Principle* (Oxford, 1986). Parts of it are technical; in particular, some of the mathematical physics might be inaccessible to nonexperts, but this drawback should not prevent anyone from understanding the full sweep of the powerful and rich new ideas about the relationship between ourselves and the cosmos, of which we are now only on the threshold. John Archibald Wheeler's *Mind in Nature* (Harper & Row, 1982) is also important.

For those who would like to approach the subject with some background first, Erwin Schrödinger's *Mind & Matter* (The University Press, 1958) is an excellent beginning, as is his beautifully written and utterly accessible little book *What Is Life?* (Cambridge University Press, 1967). Additional easy access to modern physics is Werner Heisenberg's *Physics and Philosophy* (Harper & Row, 1962) and his *Physics and Beyond* (Harper & Row, 1971). Heisenberg, famous for his Uncertainty Principle, is candid and personal about how he arrived at some of his views; particularly revealing is his account of how, after ruminating on Plato's *Timaeus*, he came to the conclusion that the ultimate constituents of everything must be not physical but mathematical.

Paul Davies, one of the best expositors of physics for the nonspecialist, wrote several books that have chapters on the Anthropic Principle. His *God and the New Physics* (Touchstone, 1984), *Edge of Infinity: Where the Universe Came From and How It Will End* (Simon & Schuster, 1981), and *Other Worlds* (Simon & Schuster, 1980), are free of equations and provide superb introductions into the mind-boggling world of quantum physics. For those who want math, his *Quantum Mechanics* (Routledge & Kegan Paul, 1984) is superb, as is his *The Accidental Universe* (Cambridge University Press, 1982).

For a whole book devoted to the question "Why is there something rather than nothing?" see Martin Heidegger's *Introduction to Metaphysics* (Doubleday, 1961), a penetrating but sometimes only marginally intelligible investigation in which the author, among other things, tries to find Being in a schoolhouse but finds only chalk. In his novel, *The Unbearable Lightness of Being*, Milan Kundera evokes the idea that Being is so insubstantial as to be almost, but not quite, nothing.

For a prominent contemporary philosopher's views on "explaining everything" and "mystical experience," see Chapter 2 of Robert Nozick's *Philosophical Explanations* (Harvard University Press, 1981).

Death

Many have claimed that all philosophy has been merely a footnote to Plato. Plato believed that life is only a reflection of another, more perfect world, to which we ascend when we die and from which we return back to this world. He invented and perfected the idea of an immaterial soul. *Phaedo* is a good place to start exploring his thoughts on death.

Martin Heidegger's *Being and Time* (Blackwell, 1967) is a difficult read but it can be thoroughly mesmerizing in a penetrating and often illuminating way. Thomas Nagel's "Birth, Death and the Meaning of Life," Chapter 11 in *The View from Nowhere* (Oxford, 1986), raises questions about what the fact of death means for us while we are alive, as does Robert Nozick in his *Philosophical Explanations* (Harvard University Press, 1981). Ian Stevenson is a psychiatrist at the University of Virginia who, in his *Twenty Cases Suggestive of Reincarnation*, 2d ed. (University Press of Virginia, 1974) provides meticulously researched and fascinating evidence of children who apparently remember their past lives.

An excellent literary but explicitly nonexistentialist approach to death is explored by Jules Romains in his novel *The Death of a Nobody* (H. Fertig, 1976). Particularly interesting is Romains's development of a social concept of a person. For a literary exploration of the absurdity of death, see Daniel Kolak's "The Wine Is in the Glass," in Kolak and Martin, eds., *The Experience of Philosophy* (Wadsworth, 1990).

Meaning

Leo Tolstoy's *Confessions* (Oxford, 1981), first published in

1905, is a moving account of a great thinker's musings on life.

The image of a man endlessly pushing a rock up a hill only to have it roll back down so that he has to push it up again has become a classic and poignant metaphor for the meaninglessness of life, epitomized by Albert Camus in *The Myth of Sisyphus and Other Essays* (Knopf, 1955). His philosophical novel on the same theme, *The Stranger*, is written in such a lucid and engaging style that many find the hero's despair downright uplifting. Jean-Paul Sartre's *Nausea* (New Directions, 1959) also explores such themes, as does his play *The Flies* (Random House, 1956) and Camus's novel *The Plague* (Random House, 1948).

The question of meaning is central to existentialist writings; for a clear and concise statement of what existentialism is, there is nothing better than Sartre's essay *Existentialism and Human Emotions* (Philosophy Library, 1957). A nice systematic account of existentialist views from Heidegger to Sartre, particularly on the effect that fear of dying has on human life, is Michael Slote's "Existentialism and the Fear of Dying" (*American Philosophical Quarterly* 12 [1975]: 17–28). For an example of a nonexistentialist approach to the subject, see Richard Taylor's "Does Life Have a Meaning?" in his *Good and Evil* (Prometheus, 1984) and Thomas Nagel's "Birth, Death and the Meaning of Life," Chapter 11 in *The View from Nowhere* (Oxford, 1986). Ludwig Wittgenstein's views on the meaning of life should not be missed; they can be found in his *Notebooks, 1914–1916* (Harper & Row, 1961), pp. 72–83, and in his *Tractatus Logico-Philosophicus* (Routledge & Kegan Paul, 1961), Sections 6.4–7. In "A Fast Car and a Good Woman," Raymond Martin questions the psychological validity of philosophical worries about the meaning of life and suggests that, as often as not, such worries merely mask a deep, underlying problem: our inability to stay satisfied; in Kolak and Martin, eds., *The Experience of Philosophy* (Wadsworth, 1990), which also contains the essays by Tolstoy, Camus, Nagel, and Taylor, already mentioned.

For those interested in psychological theories related to the problem of meaning, Victor Frankl's *Man's Search for Meaning* (Beacon, 1963) and Carl Jung's *Man in Search of a Soul*

(Harcourt Brace Jovanovich, 1955) are two very accessible classics.

For an eastern approach, Philip Kapleau's *The Three Pillars of Zen* (Anchor, 1980) is an excellent start, particularly for anyone who would appreciate sampling one form of meditation. Probably the most important and intelligible of the experiential philosophers is J. Krishnamurti. *The Awakening of Intelligence* (Harper & Row, 1976), *Think On These Things* (Harper & Row, 1964), and *Freedom from the Known* (Harper & Row, 1969) are among his best; of special interest to those who would like to see an unusual synthesis of contemporary eastern and western thought are Krishnamurti's dialogs with the physicist David Bohm in *The Ending of Time* (Harper & Row, 1985).

Ethics

The classic discussion of religious belief as a source of moral authority is Plato's *Euthyphro*. Good contemporary discussions of the same issue may be found in Antony Flew, *God and Philosophy* (Dell, 1966), Kai Nielsen, *Ethics Without God* (Prometheus Books, 1973), and Chapter 4, "Does Morality Depend on Religion?" of James Rachels's *The Elements of Moral Philosophy*, which also contains one of the best concise introductions to philosophical problems of ethics.

The 19th-century philosopher Friedrich Nietzsche mounted the fiercest attack ever on Christian morality in which he declared, "I regard Christianity as the most fatal and seductive lie that has ever yet existed—as the greatest and most *impious* lie," and urged everyone "to declare open war with it." For a good translation and selection of Nietzsche's writings, see either of Walter Kaufman's two anthologies, *The Portable Nietzsche* (Viking, 1954) or *Basic Writings of Nietzsche* (Modern Library, 1967). On the other side, Richard Swinburne's recent *Responsibility and Atonement* (Oxford University Press, 1989) is a distinguished Christian philosopher's exploration of the religious and moral meaning of merit and guilt.

On the connection between egoism and ethics, see Harry

Browne, "The Morality Trap," in his *How I Found Freedom in an Unfree World* (Macmillan, 1973), Ayn Rand, *The Virtue of Selfishness* (New American Library, 1964), Joel Feinberg, "Psychological Egoism," in his *Reason and Responsibility* (Wadsworth, 1985), Robert Olson, *The Morality of Self-Interest* (Harcourt, Brace & World, 1965), and David Gauthier, ed., *Morality and Rational Self-Interest* (Prentice-Hall, 1970).

Richard B. Brandt's "The Use of Authority in Ethics," in his *Ethical Theory* (Prentice-Hall, 1959), is excellent. On conscience as a source of moral authority, see Jonathan Bennett's delightfully disturbing essay, "The Conscience of Huckleberry Finn," in *Philosophy*, vol. 49, 1974, in which he compares the attitudes of Huckleberry Finn, the Nazi Heinrich Himmler, and the fanatical and sadistic Calvinist theologian and American religious philosopher, Jonathan Edwards.

Selections from the essays mentioned by Plato, Browne, Bennett, and Nietzsche, historically important selections by Immanuel Kant and John Stuart Mill, and Bertrand Russell's classic defense of ethical subjectivism, "Science and Ethics," are included in Kolak and Martin, eds., *The Experience of Philosophy* (Wadsworth, 1990).

Ethical relativism and the question of why anyone should be moral is discussed by Louis P. Pojman in his *Ethics: Discovering Right and Wrong* (Wadsworth, 1990). Excellent on the topic of ethical subjectivism is Bernard Williams's sophisticated but readable, *Ethics and the Limits of Philosophy* (Harvard University Press, 1985), especially Chapter 1, "Socrates' Question," Chapter 5, "Styles of Ethical Theory" and Chapter 9, "Relativism and Reflection."

A superb overview of philosophical problems of authority is Richard T. DeGeorge's *The Nature and Limits of Authority* (The University Press of Kansas, 1985), which also includes an extremely helpful bibliographic essay.

One of the best in the older generation of general anthologies on ethics is Paul Taylor, ed., *Problems of Moral Philosophy* (Wadsworth, 1978). Richard Brandt, *Value and Obligation* (Harcourt, Brace & World, 1961), John Hospers, *Human Conduct* (Harcourt, Brace & World, 1961), and

William Frankena's concise, *Ethics* (Prentice-Hall, 1963), though somewhat dated now, are still valuable introductory texts. All four have been used so widely that there is a good chance you can find them in your university library.

Excellent more recent anthologies include Louis Pojman, ed., *Ethical Theory* (Wadsworth, 1989) and Jonathan Glover, ed., *Utilitarianism and Its Critics* (Macmillan, 1990). For a nonutilitarian approach, see Bernard Gert's *Morality: A New Justification of the Moral Rules* (Oxford, 1988).

Applied ethics has been a growth industry for the last two decades, and many good anthologies and texts are now available. Joan Callahan's excellently edited collection, *Ethical Issues in Professional Life* (Oxford University Press, 1988) is one of the best. Other good sources include Richard M. Fox and Joseph P. DeMarco, eds., *Moral Reasoning: A Philosophical Approach to Applied Ethics* (Holt, Rinehart and Winston, 1989), W. Michael Hoffman and Jennifer M. Moore, eds., *Business Ethics* (McGraw-Hill, 1990), Holmes Rolston, III, *Environmental Ethics* (Temple University Press, 1990), Pablo Iannone, ed., *Contemporary Moral Controversies in Technology* (Oxford University Press, 1987) and, on ethical problems in journalism, Anthony Serafini, ed., *Ethics and Social Concern* (Paragon House, 1990).

Values

On the distinction between fact and value, see any of the ethics anthologies and texts just mentioned or David B. Wong, ed., *Moral Relativity* (University of California, 1984). Thomas Nagel defends the objectivity of values in "The Limits of Objectivity," in *The Tanner Lectures on Human Values*, edited by Sterling M. McMurrin (University of Utah Press, 1980) and in his *The View From Nowhere* (Oxford University Press, 1986).

For interesting and influential defenses of ethical and valuational subjectivity, see Jean-Paul Sartre's classic, *Existentialism* (Philosophical Library, 1957), and J. L. Mackie's more analytic, *Ethics: Inventing Right and Wrong* (Harmondsworth: Penguin, 1977).

Sartre's views are sympathetically criticized and then

creatively developed by Charles Taylor in "Responsibility for Self," in Amélie O. Rorty, ed., *The Identities of Persons* (University of California Press, 1976). Taylor continues to develop his view in his *Sources of the Self* (Harvard University Press, 1990). Mary Midgley, in *Wisdom, Information & Wonder* (Routledge, 1989) has some interesting criticisms of existentialist theories of value as well as a powerfully expressed alternative view of her own. Mackie's views are criticized by David O. Brink in, "Moral Realism and the Skeptical Arguments from Disagreement and Queerness," *Australasian Journal of Philosophy*, vol. 62, 1984.

The development of our views in the present chapter on eliminating ethics and values owes a great deal to recent work by Richard Garner, especially his "On the Genuine Queerness of Moral Properties and Facts," *Australasian Journal of Philosophy*, v. 68, 1990, "Nagel on the Badness of Pain," (unpublished), and his book-in-progress, tentatively entitled *Beyond Morality*.

On the idea that we can get out from under our current frameworks of values and get a worthwhile perspective on them meditatively, that is, by just watching our thoughts and behavior, see Sujata's charming little book of epigrams and cartoons, *Beginning to See* (Apple Pie Books, 1983), Joseph Goldstein's manual for insight-meditation, *The Experience of Insight* (Unity Press, 1976), and Shunryu Suzuki's classic *Zen Mind, Beginner's Mind* (Weatherhill, 1970).

Self-deception is expertly discussed in Herbert Fingarette's readable, *Self-Deception* (Humanities Press, 1969), Mary Haight's *A Study of Self-Deception* (Humanities Press, 1980), Mark W. Martin's two anthologies, *Self-Deception and Self-Understanding: New Essays in Philosophy and Psychology* (University Press of Kansas, 1985), and *Self-Deception and Morality* (University Press of Kansas, 1986), and Brian McLaughlin and Amélie O. Rorty, eds., *Perspectives on Self-Deception* (University of California, 1988).

Interesting feminist perspectives on values may be found in Simone De Beauvoir, *The Second Sex* (Penguin, 1976), Simone Weil, "Friendship," in *Waiting for God* (Harper & Row, 1983), Adrienne Rich, "Women and Honor: Some Notes on Lying," in her *On Lies, Secrets, and Silence, Selected Prose 1966-1978* (W. W. Norton, 1979), Kate Millet, *Sexual Politics* (Doubleday, 1970), Joan Roberts, ed., *Beyond Intellectual Sexism: A New Woman, A New Reality* (David McKay, 1976), Joan Kelley, *Women, History, and Theory* (University of Chicago Press, 1984), and Marilyn Pearsall, *Women and Values* (Wadsworth, 1986).

The impact of recent and possible technology on values is engagingly discussed by Jonathan Glover in *What Sort of People Should There Be?* (Penguin, 1984).

Bertrand Russell's "The Value of Philosophy," in his *Problems of Philosophy* (Oxford University Press, 1912), is a classic. Excerpts from several of the works mentioned here, including those by Sartre, Rich, Glover and Russell, are to be found in Kolak and Martin, eds., *The Experience of Philosophy* (Wadsworth, 1990).